Creepy Crawly
ANIMAL
ORIGAMI

Duy Nguyen

CONTRA COSTA COUNTY LIBRARY
Sterling Publishing Co. Inc.

3 1901 04310 1916

Design by Judy Morgan
Edited by Claire Bazinet

Library of Congress Cataloging-in-Publication Data
Nguyen, Duy, 1960-
  Creepy crawly animal origami / Duy Nguyen.
     p. cm.
  Includes index.
  ISBN 0-8069-9012-0
  1. Origami. 2. Insects in art. 3. Reptiles in art. 4. Origami. I. Title.
TT870 .N48595 2003
736'.982--dc21

                             2002015507

10 9 8 7 6 5 4 3 2 1

Published in paperback in 2005 by Sterling Publishing Co., Inc.
387 Park Avenue South, New York, NY 10016
© 2003 by Duy Nguyen
Distributed in Canada by Sterling Publishing
C/o Canadian Manda Group, 165 Dufferin Street
Toronto, Ontario, Canada M6K 3H6
Distributed in Great Britain and Europe by Chris Lloyd at Orca Book
Services, Stanley House, Fleets Lane, Poole BH15 3AJ, England
Distributed in Australia by Capricorn Link (Australia) Pty. Ltd.
P.O. Box 704, Windsor, NSW 2756, Australia
Printed in China
All rights reserved

Sterling ISBN 0-8069-9012-0 Hardcover
       ISBN 1-4027-2229-X Paperback

Contents

Preface

Traditionally, a person practicing "origami" works with only a single square sheet of paper, with no cutting and pasting. The idea is to express oneself creatively wholly through the art of folding paper—and folding paper exclusively. This often means, however, that finished traditional origami projects, although pleasing in their simplicity and esthetically beautiful, may have a two-dimensional look. The creations may not even be recognizable.

In each of my origami books, I strongly suggest that readers allow themselves the freedom to be fully creative in completing a project and to strive for a natural look. It is even more important for the creepy crawly subjects of this book. The completed origami insects or reptiles here are rendered only more attractive by giving them "movement" and surroundings that complement them. An alligator, for example, becomes much more alive with a slight turn of the head and an opposite curve in the tail. Army ants aligned with others on a realistic origami (or real) tree branch come quickly to life, "marching" with purpose in their natural habitat. Touches of paint or pasted-on detail can also work wonders creatively.

So, with realism in mind, understand that the completed origami that you create from this book, or from other books on origami, do not need to look exactly like the illustrations you see. Origami creations are waiting for you yourself to give them "life"—with all its abundant variety.

Duy Nguyen

Introduction

Origami is known as the art of paper folding so it is no surprise that much traditional origami is confined to the simple folding of paper to form objects. I have noticed, however, that although origami originated in Japan, many Japanese origami books allow, if not encourage, cutting and pasting in the creation of different origami pieces. This makes creating origami figures much easier and allows a greater number of enthusiasts to involve themselves in working out new and original forms, not merely repeating the same step-by-step instructions from books.

To me and to many other Origami "traditionalists," cutting and pasting are important tools to designing and capturing a taste of realism in paper creations—resulting in new and original origami that is more realistic. When it come to creativity, one should never let unnecessary rules form barriers or make things more complicated than needed. After all, if strict origami paper is not available, the first activity in starting an origami project is to find any usable paper, pasting strips together if necessary, and cutting it into a square or any other shape required to work out the figure. Why, at that point, bind ourselves strictly to paper-folding? How much cutting and pasting are too much? In practicing the art of origami, advancing creativity is much more important than simple repetition.

A word here of encouragement. When I first began learning origami, I struggled with even the simplest folds, such as the valley, mountain and pleat folds. When trying to fold an object, I had to look back at the opening chapter again and again to review these basic folds and how to do them. I would also look ahead, at the diagram showing the next step of whatever project I was folding, to see how it *should* look, to be sure that I was following the instructions correctly. Looking ahead at the "next step," the result of a fold, is a very good way for a beginner to learn origami.

Another way to make learning origami easier is to create "construction lines" before doing a complex fold. By this I mean to pre-fold, then unfold, to crease the form and create guidelines. For example: when getting ready to fold a pleat fold reverse or inside and outside reverse folds, if you pre-crease, by using mountain and valley folds, the finished fold is more likely to match the one shown in the book. When your finished folds look different, due to fold lines being at slightly different angles, it can cause confusion and throw you off. It is also important to make good clean fold lines. Well-made construction lines are helpful when you want to unfold the form slightly in order to make another fold easier.

By using these learning techniques, you should have no problem catching on to the basics of origami and performing folds with a minimum of mistakes. The step-by-step instructions and clearly marked folds given here will quickly have you handcrafting a houseful of creepy crawly friends.

Basic Instructions

Paper: The best paper to use for traditional origami is very thin, keeps a crease well, and folds flat. You can use plain white paper, solid-color paper, or wrapping paper with a design only on one side. Be aware, though, that some kinds of paper stretch slightly, either in length or in width, while others tear easily. Packets of papers especially for use in origami (15 by 15 centimeters square, or a bit under 6 by 6 inches) are available in a variety of colors from craft and hobby shops.

Regular typing paper may be too heavy to allow for the many tight folds needed in creating more complex, traditional, origami figures, but it should be fine for several of the larger papercraft works, with fewer folds, given here. For those who are learning and have a problem getting their fingers to work tight folds, larger paper sizes are fine. Slightly larger figures are easier to make than overly small ones.

Glue: Use a good, easy-flowing but not loose paper glue, but use it sparingly. You don't want to soak the paper. A toothpick makes a good applicator. Allow the glued form time to dry. Avoid using stick glue, as the application pressure needed (especially if the stick has become dry) can damage your figure.

Technique: Fold with care. Position the paper, especially at corners, precisely and see that edges line up before creasing a fold. Once you are sure of the fold, use a fingernail to make a clean, flat crease. Don't get discouraged with your first efforts. In time, what your mind can create, your fingers can fashion.

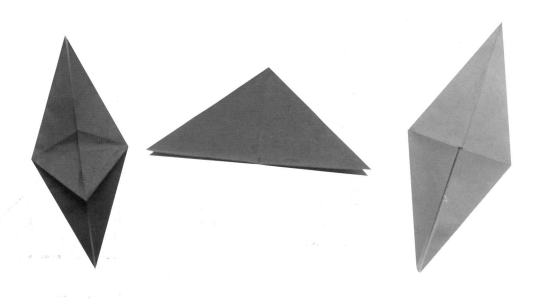

Symbols & Lines

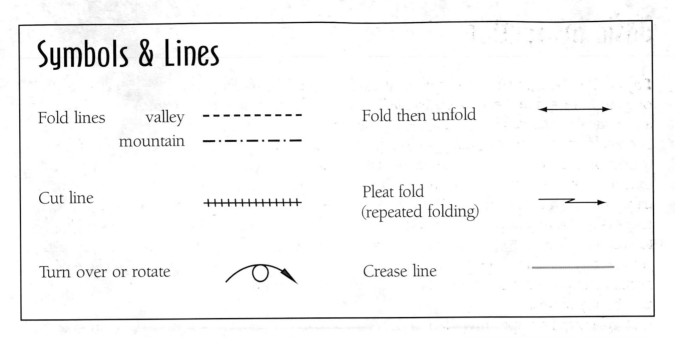

Fold lines   valley   - - - - - - - - -   Fold then unfold

mountain   - - - - - - -

Cut line   ++++++++++++   Pleat fold
(repeated folding)

Turn over or rotate   Crease line

Squaring-Off Paper

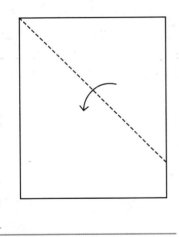

1

Take a rectangular sheet
of paper and valley fold it
diagonally to opposite edge.

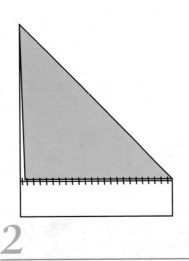

2

Cut off excess on long side
as shown.

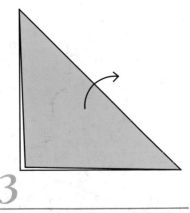

3

Unfold, and sheet is square.

Basic Folds

Kite Fold

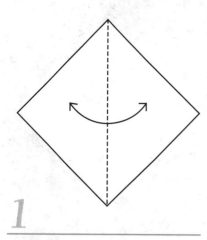

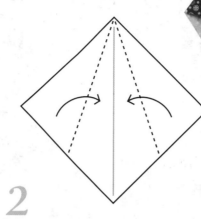

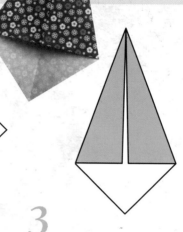

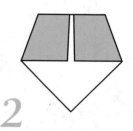

1
Fold and unfold a square diagonally, making a center crease.

2
Fold both sides in to the center crease.

3
This is a kite form.

Valley Fold   - - - - - - - - - -

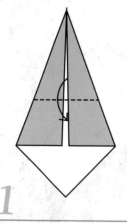

1
Here, using the kite, fold form toward you (forward), making a "valley."

2
This fold forward is a valley fold.

Mountain Fold   —·—·—·—·—

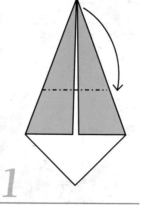

1
Here, using the kite, fold form away from you (backwards), making a "mountain."

2
This fold backwards is a mountain fold.

Inside Reverse Fold

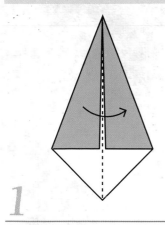

1
Starting here with a kite, valley fold kite closed.

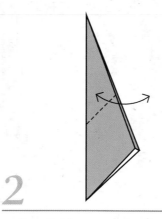

2
Valley fold as marked to crease, then unfold.

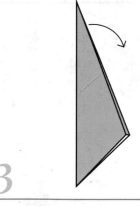

3
Pull tip in direction of arrow.

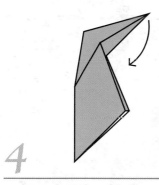

4
Appearance before completion.

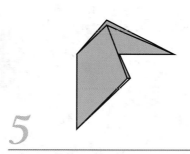

5
You've made an inside reverse fold.

Outside Reverse Fold

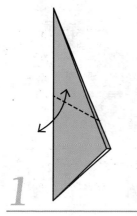

1
Using closed kite, valley fold, unfold.

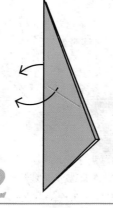

2
Fold inside out, as shown by arrows.

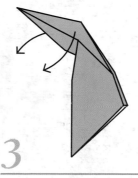

3
Appearance before completion.

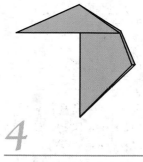

4
You've made an outside reverse fold.

Basic Folds

Pleat Fold

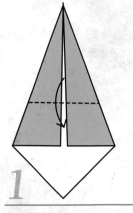

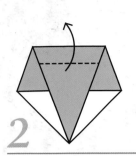

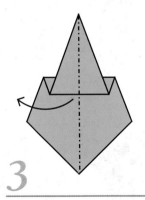

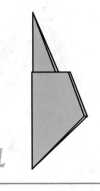

1 Here, using the kite, valley fold.

2 Valley fold back again.

3 This is a pleat. Valley fold in half.

4 You've made a pleat fold.

Pleat Fold Reverse

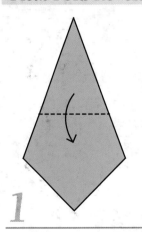

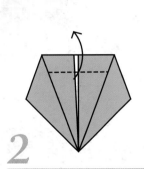

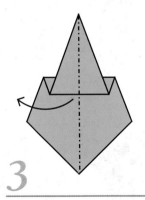

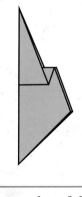

1 Here, using the kite form backwards, valley fold.

2 Valley fold back again for pleat.

3 Mountain fold form in half.

4 This is a pleat fold reverse.

Squash Fold I

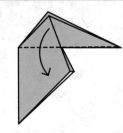

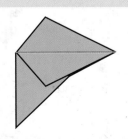

1 Using inside reverse, valley fold one side.

2 This is a squash fold I.

Squash Fold II

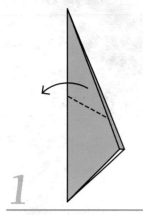

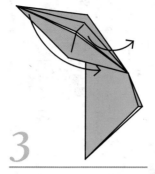

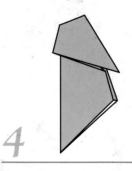

1
Using closed kite form, valley fold.

2
Open in direction of the arrow.

3
Appearance before completion.

4
You've made a squash fold II.

Inside Crimp Fold

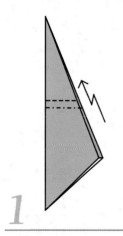

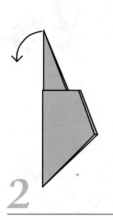

1
Here using closed kite form, pleat fold.

2
Pull tip in direction of the arrow.

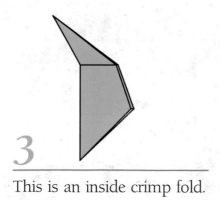

3
This is an inside crimp fold.

Outside Crimp Fold

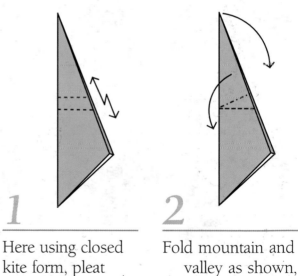

1
Here using closed kite form, pleat fold and unfold.

2
Fold mountain and valley as shown, both sides.

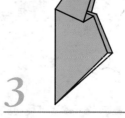

3
This is an outside crimp fold.

Base Folds

Base folds are basic forms that do not in themselves produce origami, but serve as a basis, or jumping-off point, for a number of creative origami figures, some quite complex. As when beginning other crafts, learning to fold these base folds is not the most exciting part of origami. They are, however, easy to do, and will help you with your technique. They also quickly become rote, so much so that you can do many using different-colored papers while you are watching television or your mind is elsewhere. With completed base folds handy, if you want to quickly work up a form or are suddenly inspired with an idea for an original, unique figure, you can select an appropriate base fold and swiftly bring a new creation to life.

Base Fold I

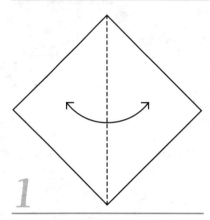

1
Fold and unfold in direction of arrow.

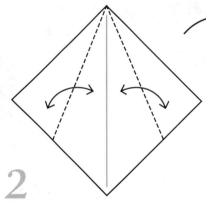

2
Fold both sides in to center crease, then unfold. Rotate.

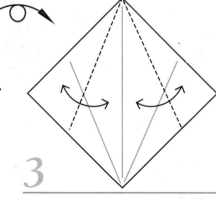

3
Fold both sides in to center crease, then unfold.

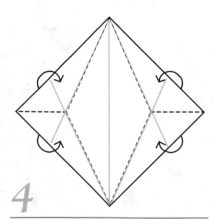

4
Pinch corners of square together and fold inward.

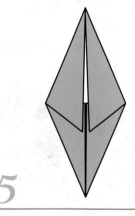

5
Completed Base Fold I.

Base Folds

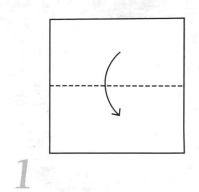

1

Valley fold.

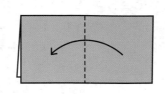

2

Valley fold.

3

Squash fold.

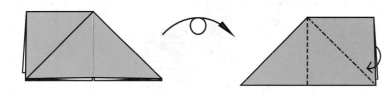

4

Turn over to other side.

5

Squash fold.

6

Completed Base Fold II.

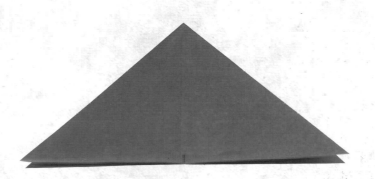

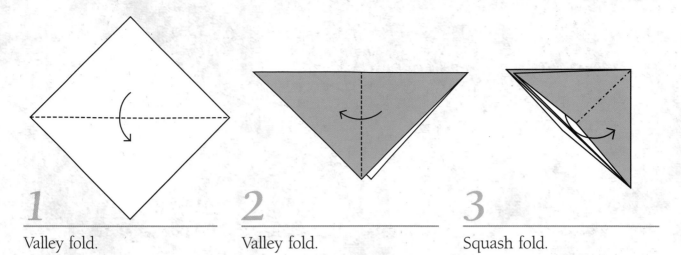

1

Valley fold.

2

Valley fold.

3

Squash fold.

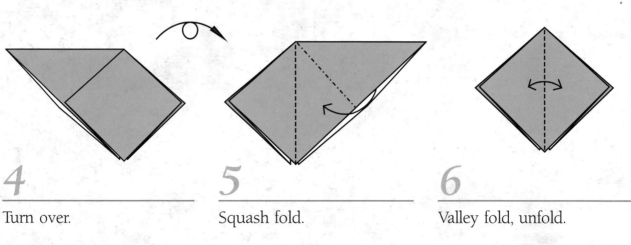

4

Turn over.

5

Squash fold.

6

Valley fold, unfold.

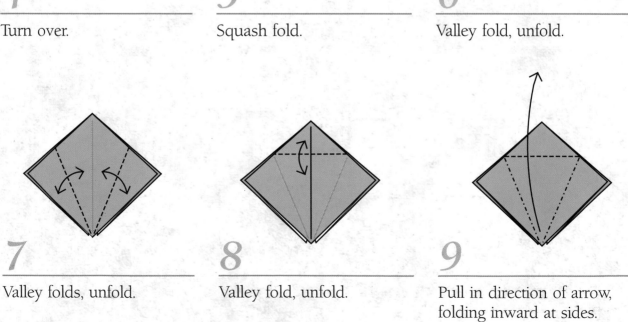

7

Valley folds, unfold.

8

Valley fold, unfold.

9

Pull in direction of arrow, folding inward at sides.

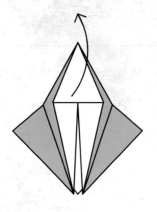

10

Appearance before
completion of fold.

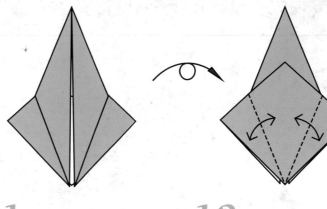

11

Fold completed. Turn over.

12

Valley folds, unfold.

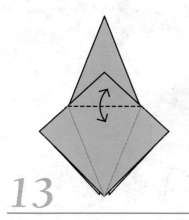

13

Valley fold, unfold.

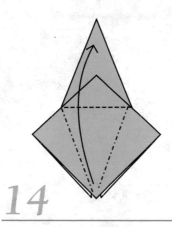

14

Repeat, again pulling in
direction of arrow.

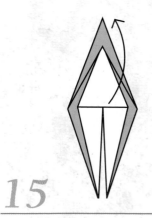

15

Appearance before
completion.

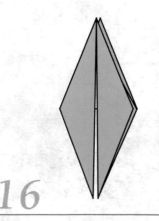

16

Completed Base Fold III.

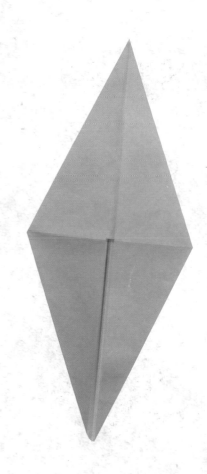

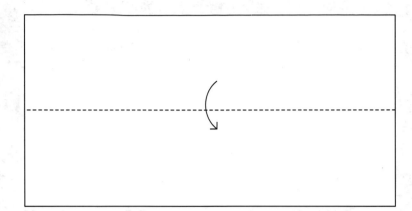

1

Valley fold rectangular size paper (length variable) in half as shown.

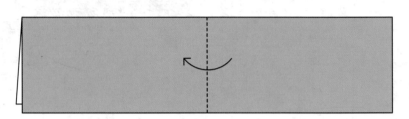

2

Valley fold in direction of arrow.

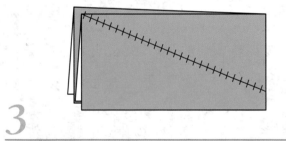

3

Make cut as shown.

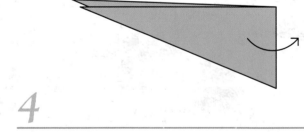

4

Unfold.

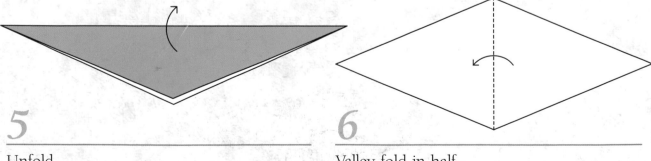

5

Unfold.

6

Valley fold in half.

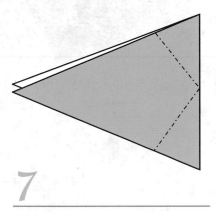

7

Inside reverse folds to inner center crease.

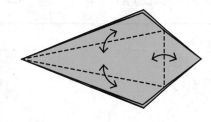

8

Valley fold and unfold to crease.

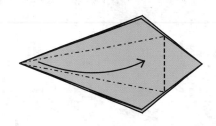

9

Pull in direction of arrow, and fold.

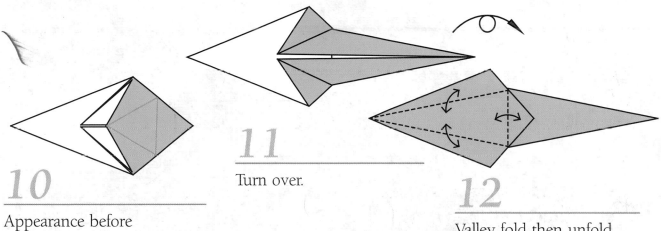

10

Appearance before completion.

11

Turn over.

12

Valley fold then unfold.

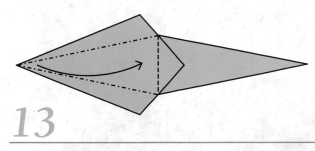

13

Again, pull in direction of arrow, and fold.

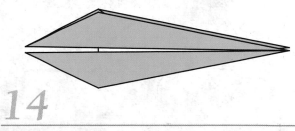

14

Completed Base Fold IV.

Scorpion

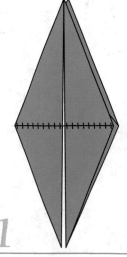

1 Start with Base Fold III. Cuts to top layer.

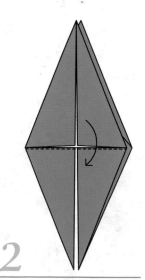

2 Valley fold.

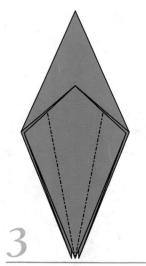

3 Inside reverse folds.

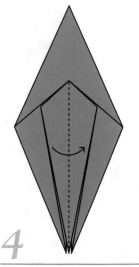

4 Valley fold.

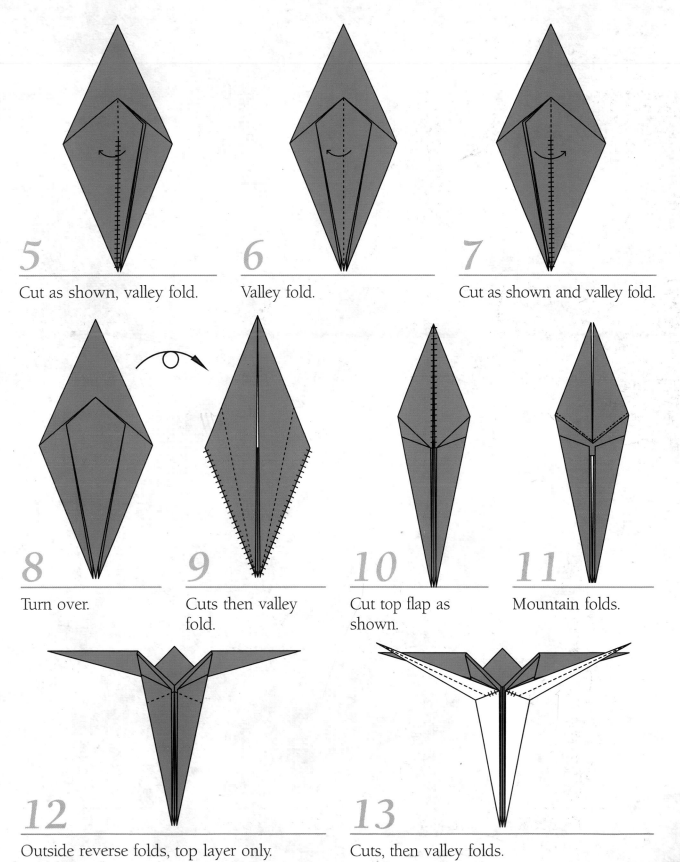

5 Cut as shown, valley fold.

6 Valley fold.

7 Cut as shown and valley fold.

8 Turn over.

9 Cuts then valley fold.

10 Cut top flap as shown.

11 Mountain folds.

12 Outside reverse folds, top layer only.

13 Cuts, then valley folds.

Scorpion

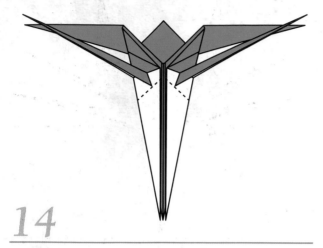

14

Outside reverse fold.

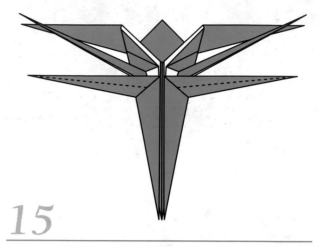

15

Valley folds both sides.

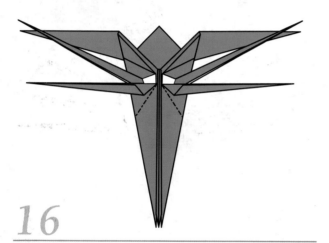

16

Mountain folds.

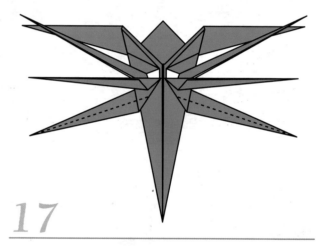

17

Valley folds.

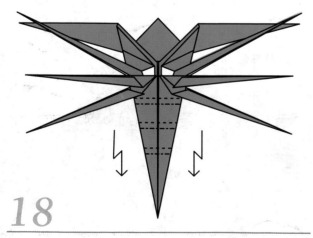

18

Pleat folds.

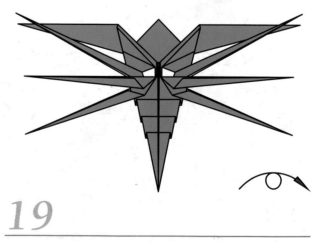

19

Turn over to other side.

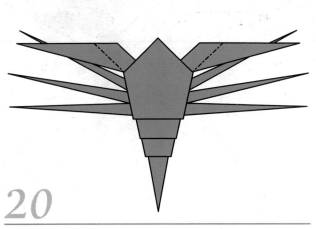

20

Mountain folds.

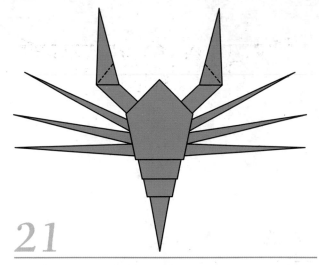

21

Inside reverse folds.

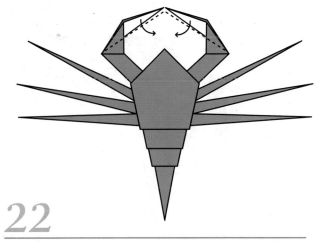

22

Valley folds.

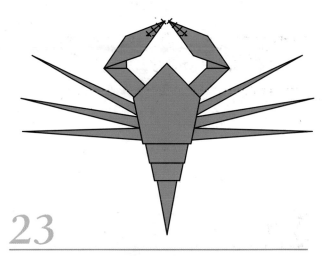

23

Cuts as shown. Mountain fold sections of cut parts.

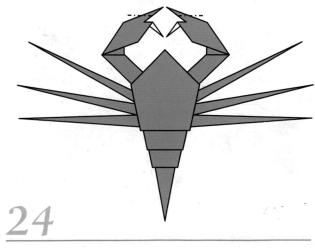

24

Mountain folds.

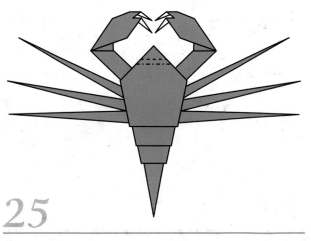

25

Pleat fold.

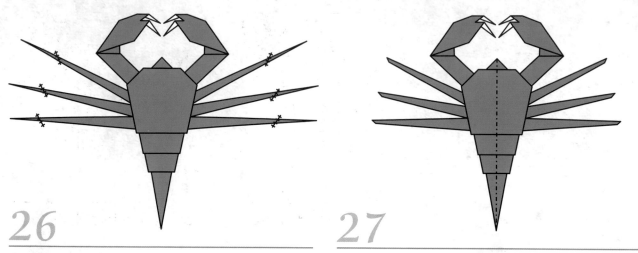

26

Cuts as shown.

27

Mountain fold in half

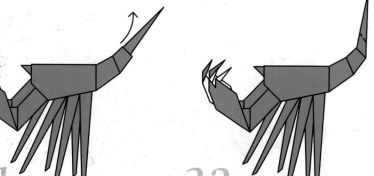

28

Rotate.

29

Pull and crimp/squash first fold into position.

30

Pull and crimp/squash second fold into position.

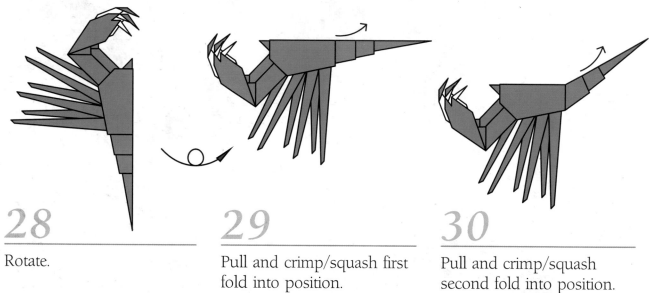

31

Pull and crimp/squash third fold into position.

32

Outside reverse fold.

33

Cuts and valley folds.

34

Inside reverse fold tail.

35

Inside reverse fold again.

36

Fold and unfold claws.

37

Open out form and pleat
fold legs, front and back.

38

Completed Scorpion.

Alligator

Part 1

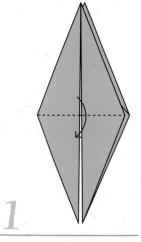

1
Start with Base Fold III, valley fold.

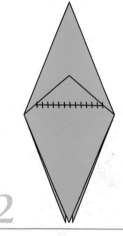

2
Cut as shown.

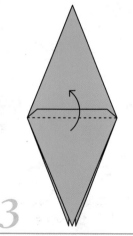

3
Valley fold.

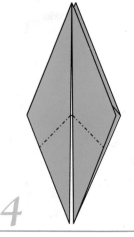

4
Inside reverse folds.

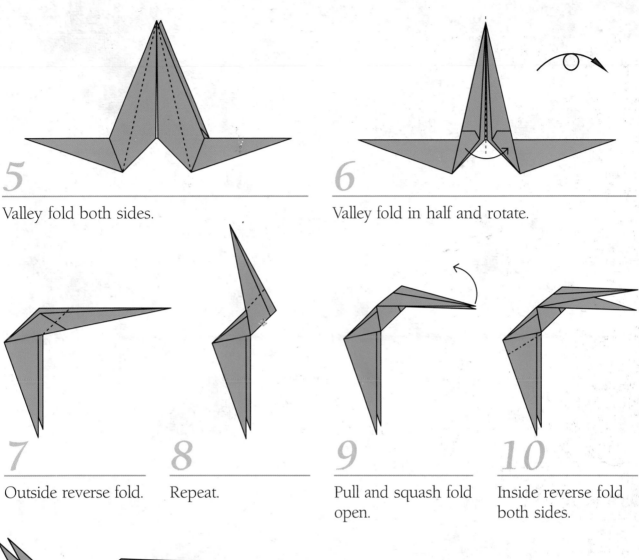

5

Valley fold both sides.

6

Valley fold in half and rotate.

7

Outside reverse fold.

8

Repeat.

9

Pull and squash fold open.

10

Inside reverse fold both sides.

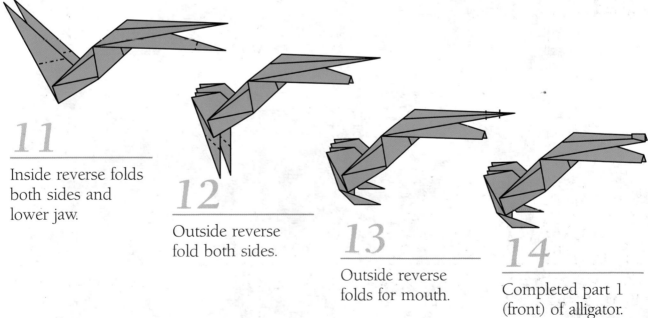

11

Inside reverse folds both sides and lower jaw.

12

Outside reverse fold both sides.

13

Outside reverse folds for mouth.

14

Completed part 1 (front) of alligator.

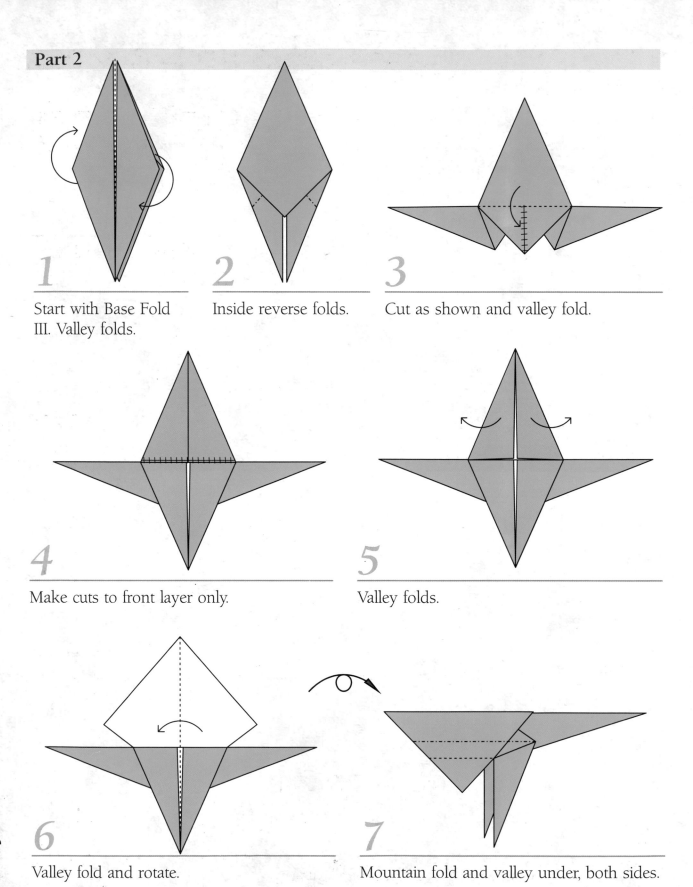

1
Start with Base Fold III. Valley folds.

2
Inside reverse folds.

3
Cut as shown and valley fold.

4
Make cuts to front layer only.

5
Valley folds.

6
Valley fold and rotate.

7
Mountain fold and valley under, both sides.

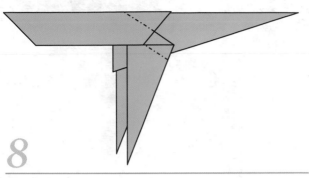

8

Inside reverse fold both sides.

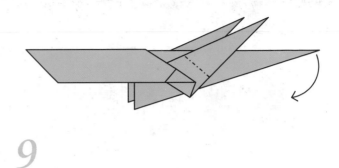

9

Inside reverse fold both sides, then pull and squash fold tail into position.

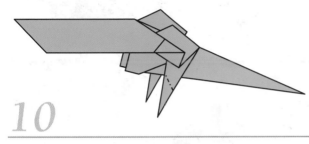

10

Inside reverse fold both front and back.

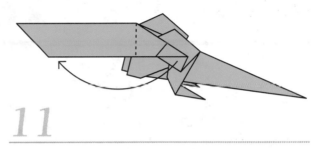

11

Valley fold both front and back.

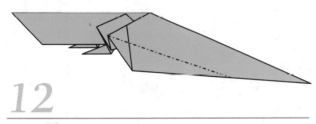

12

Mountain fold both front and back.

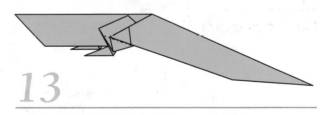

13

Mountain fold both front and back.

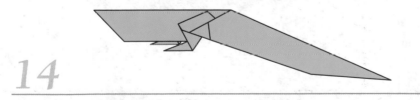

14

Completed part 2 (rear) of alligator.

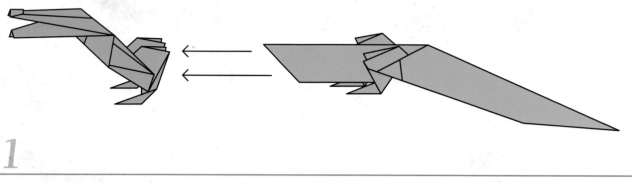

1

Join parts 1 and 2 together as shown and apply glue to hold. Press and pull the tail into a natural-looking curve.

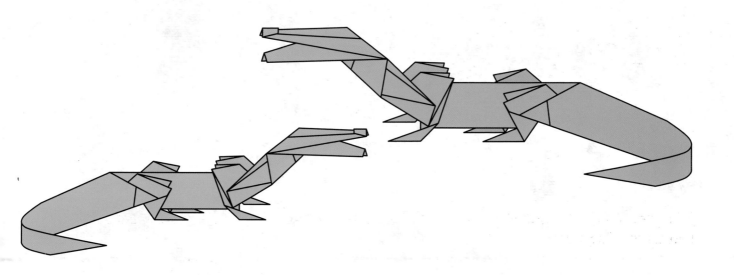

2

Completed Alligator.

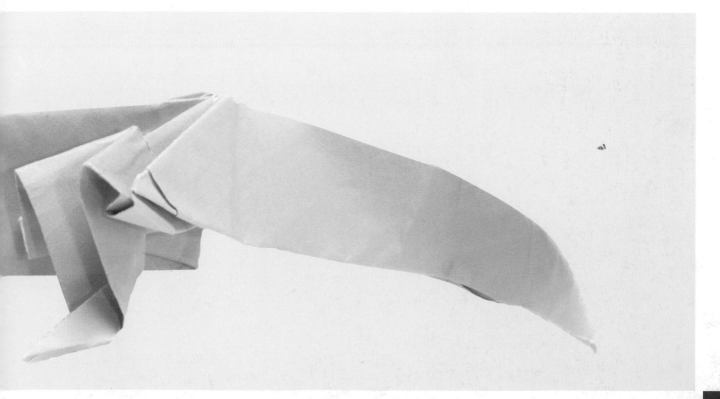

Dragonfly

Part 1

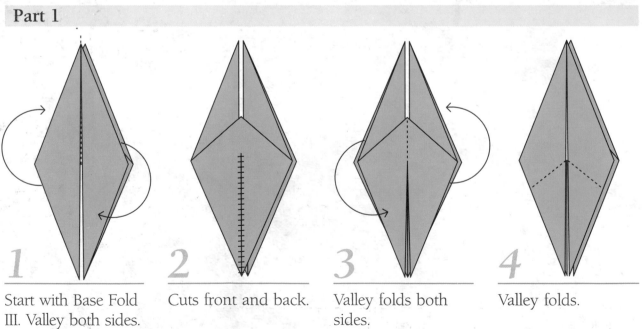

1
Start with Base Fold III. Valley both sides.

2
Cuts front and back.

3
Valley folds both sides.

4
Valley folds.

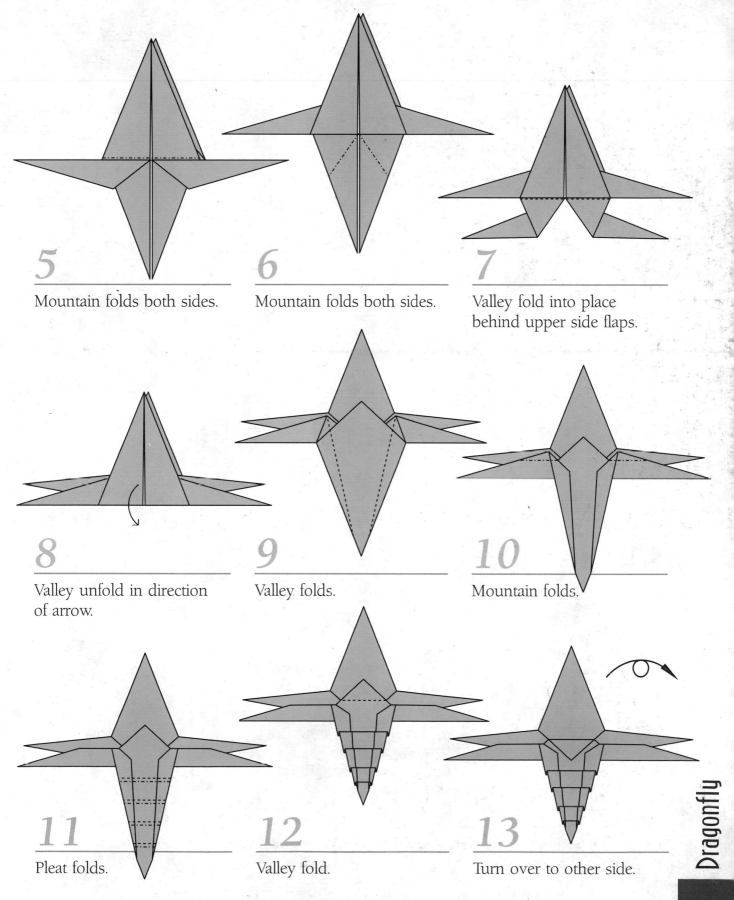

5

Mountain folds both sides.

6

Mountain folds both sides.

7

Valley fold into place behind upper side flaps.

8

Valley unfold in direction of arrow.

9

Valley folds.

10

Mountain folds.

11

Pleat folds.

12

Valley fold.

13

Turn over to other side.

14

Squash folds.

15

Mountain folds.

16

Mountain fold in half, then rotate.

17

Cut through as shown.

18

Mountain fold, both sides.

19

Outside reverse fold.

20

Repeat outside reverse.

21

Outside reverse fold.

22

Outside reverse fold.

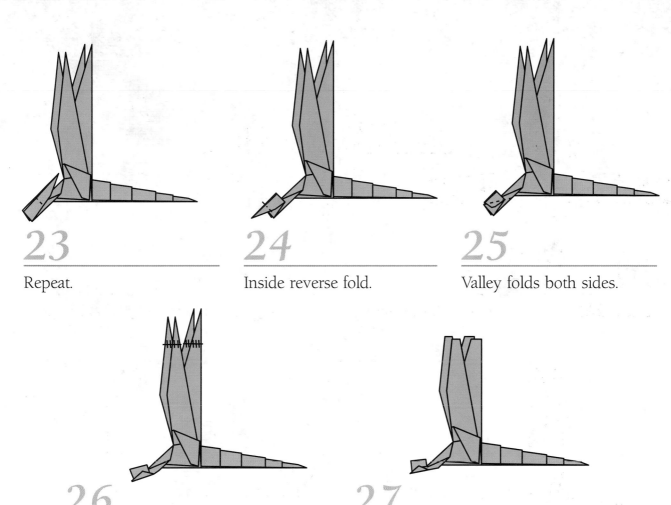

23

Repeat.

24

Inside reverse fold.

25

Valley folds both sides.

26

Make cuts as shown.

27

Complete part 1 (front) of dragonfly.

Part 2

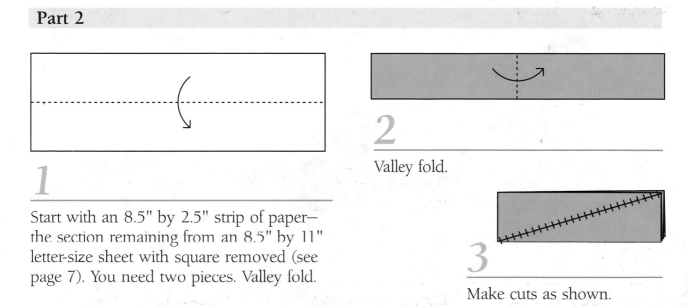

1

Start with an 8.5" by 2.5" strip of paper—
the section remaining from an 8.5" by 11"
letter-size sheet with square removed (see
page 7). You need two pieces. Valley fold.

2

Valley fold.

3

Make cuts as shown.

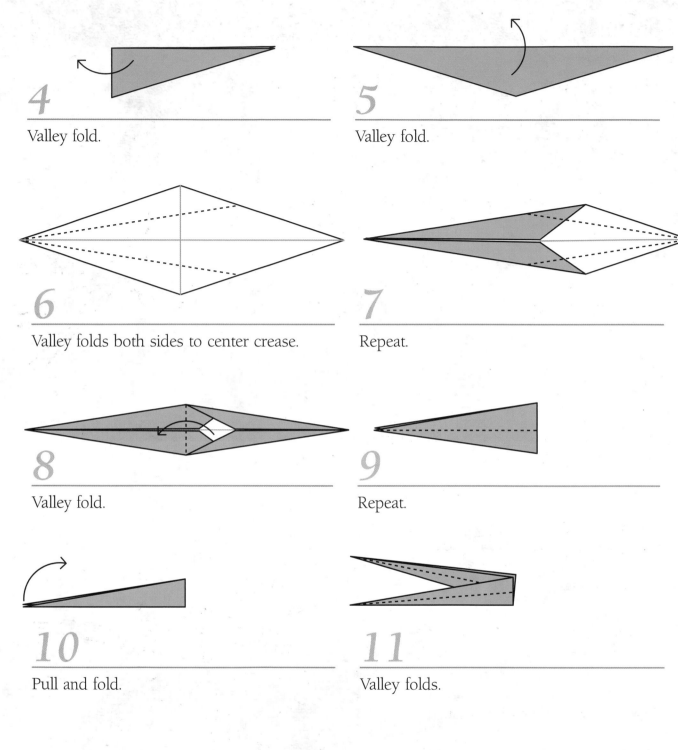

4

Valley fold.

5

Valley fold.

6

Valley folds both sides to center crease.

7

Repeat.

8

Valley fold.

9

Repeat.

10

Pull and fold.

11

Valley folds.

12

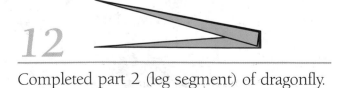

Completed part 2 (leg segment) of dragonfly.

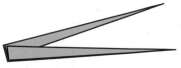

Make another, for two.

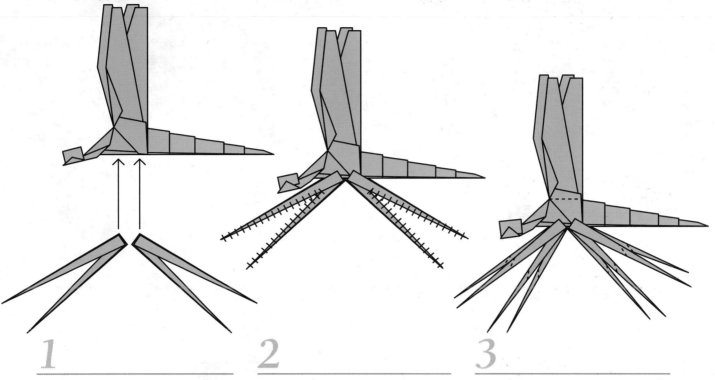

1
Join leg segments to body as shown. Apply glue to hold.

2
Make cuts as shown.

3
Valley folds.

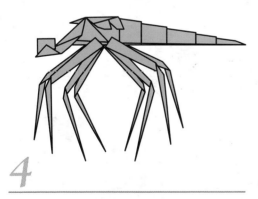

4
Position legs for standing position.

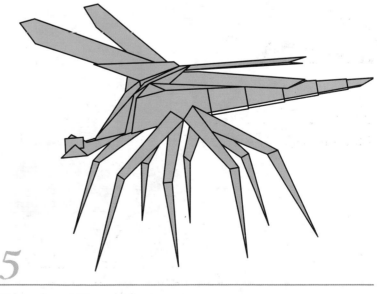

5
Completed Dragonfly.

Lobster

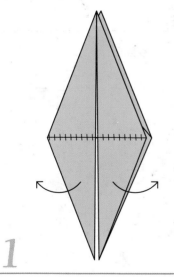

1

Start with Base Fold III. Cut front layer, then unfold.

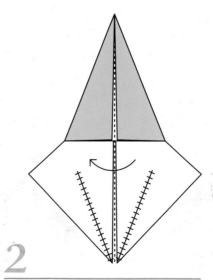

2

Cut as shown, then valley fold in half

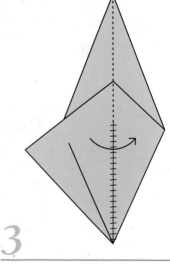

3

Cut as shown, then valley fold back.

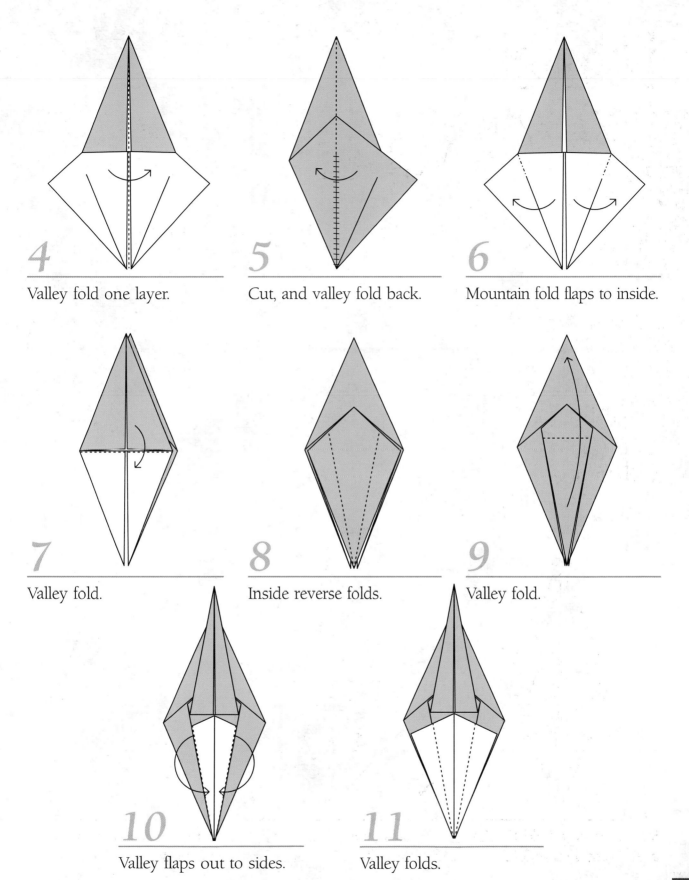

4

Valley fold one layer.

5

Cut, and valley fold back.

6

Mountain fold flaps to inside.

7

Valley fold.

8

Inside reverse folds.

9

Valley fold.

10

Valley flaps out to sides.

11

Valley folds.

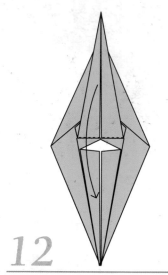

12

Valley fold.

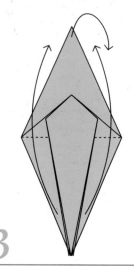

13

Valley side flaps upward, and back downward.

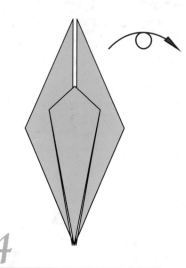

14

Turn over.

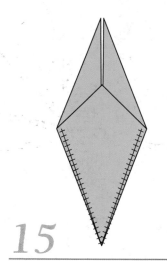

15

Cut side strips as shown.

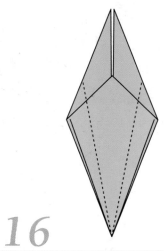

16

Valley folds.

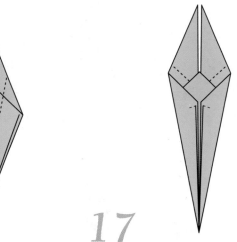

17

Valley folds.

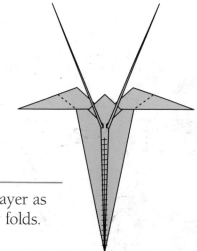

18

Cut through layer as shown, valley folds.

19

Outside reverse folds.

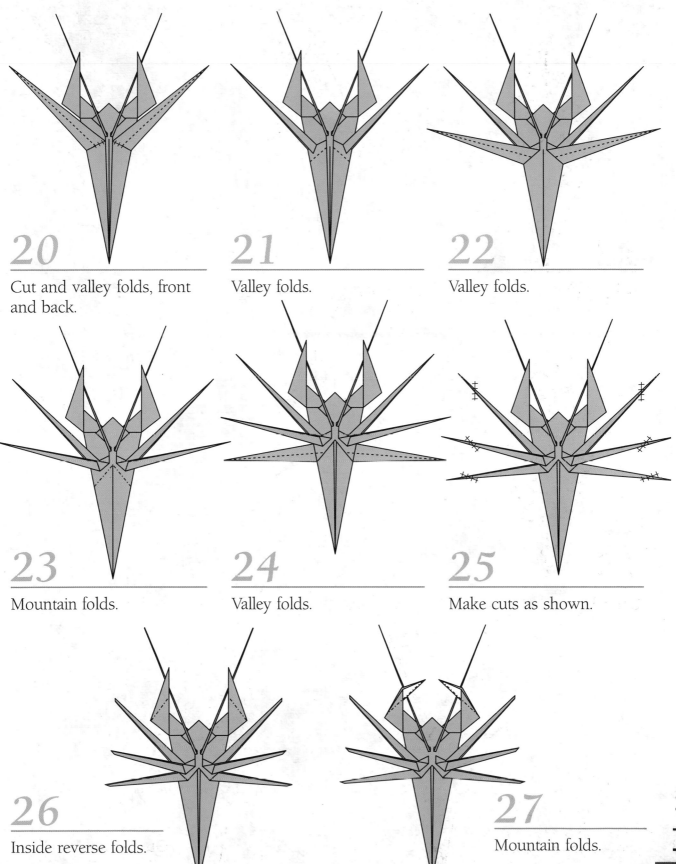

20

Cut and valley folds, front and back.

21

Valley folds.

22

Valley folds.

23

Mountain folds.

24

Valley folds.

25

Make cuts as shown.

26

Inside reverse folds.

27

Mountain folds.

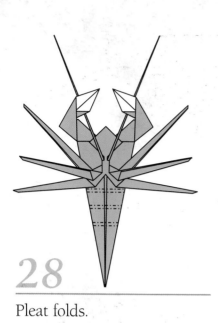

28

Pleat folds.

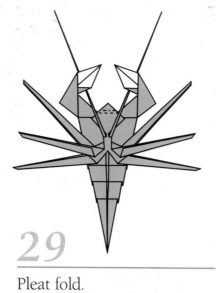

29

Pleat fold.

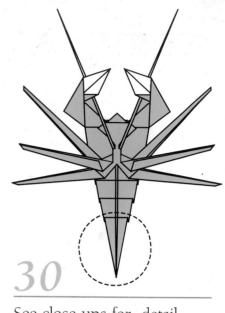

30

See close-ups for detail.

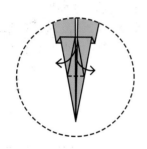

31

Squash folds.

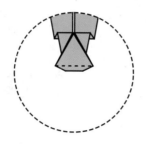

32

Valley fold.

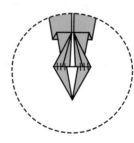

33

Cuts as shown.

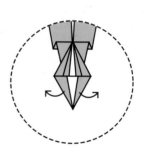

34

Unfold to sides.

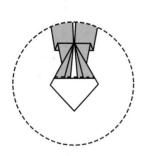

35

Valley fold.

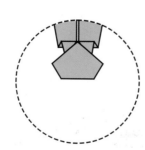

36

Return to full view.

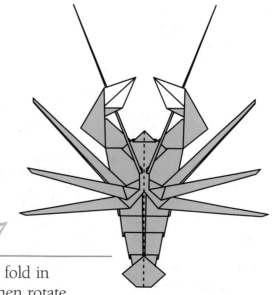

37

Valley fold in
half, then rotate.

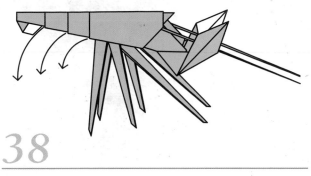

38

Pull tail section folds into position as shown.

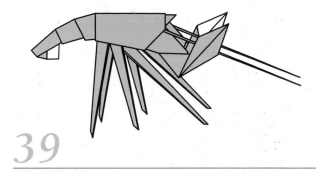

39

Valley fold both antennae to rear.

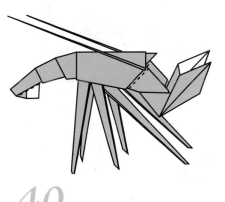

40

Valley fold both sides.

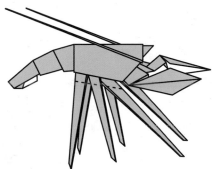

41

Valley fold both sides.

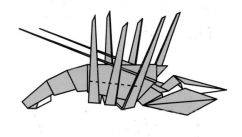

42

Valley fold both sides, and position legs for standing.

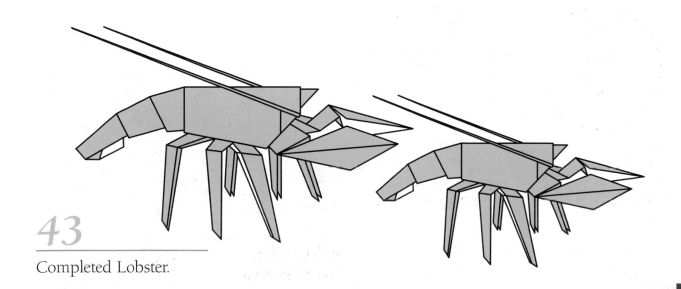

43

Completed Lobster.

Gecko

Part 1

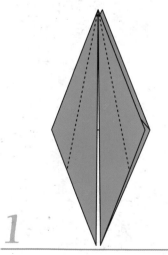

1

Start with Base Fold III.
Valley fold.

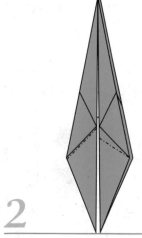

2

Inside reverse folds both
right and left.

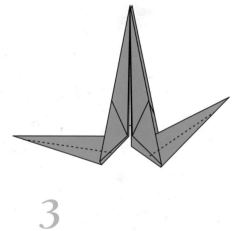

3

Valley folds.

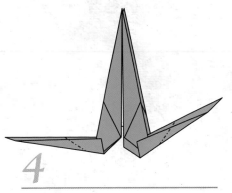

4
Inside reverse folds.

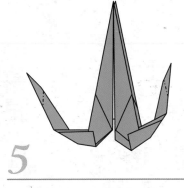

5
Inside reverse folds.

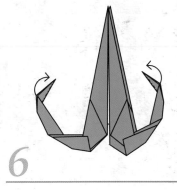

6
Mountain folds.

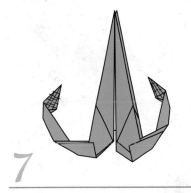

7
Make cuts (3 on each foot).

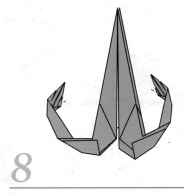

8
Mountain fold outer "toes."

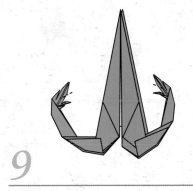

9
Repeat mountain folds.

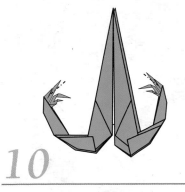

10
Mountain folds again.

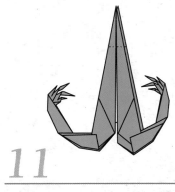

11
Mountain fold, front and back.

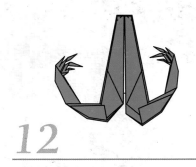

12
Valley folds.

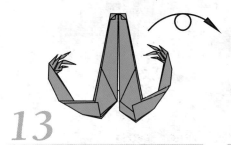

13
Turn over to other side.

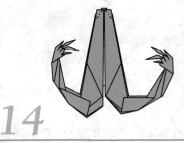

14
Mountain folds.

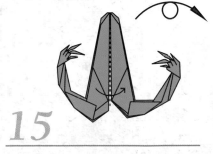

15
Valley fold in half and rotate.

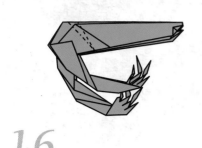

16

Pleat fold.

17

Inside reverse fold.

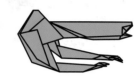

18

Valley folds.

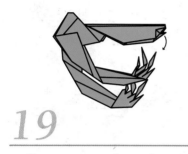

19

Pull open mouth and crimp lower jaw into position.

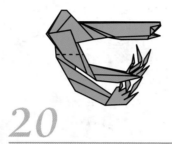

20

Valley fold "toes."

21

Completed part 1 (front) of gecko.

Part 2

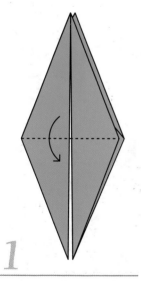

1

Start with Base Fold III.

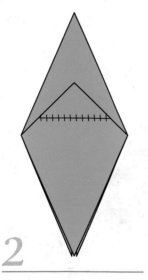

2

Cuts, then turn over.

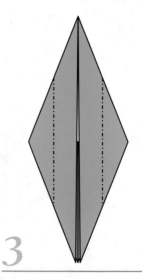

3

Mountain folds.

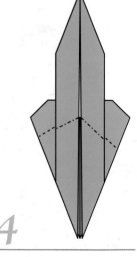

4

Inside reverse folds.

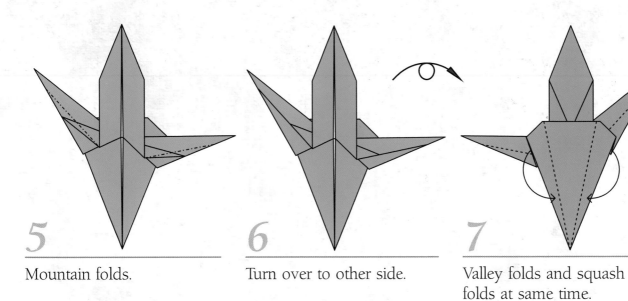

5
Mountain folds.

6
Turn over to other side.

7
Valley folds and squash
folds at same time.

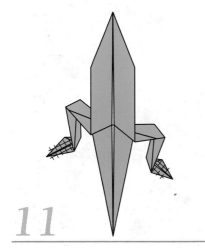

8
Turn over.

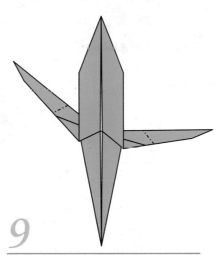

9
Mountain folds.

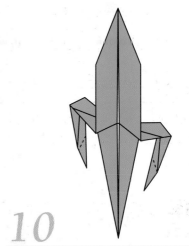

10
Squash folds.

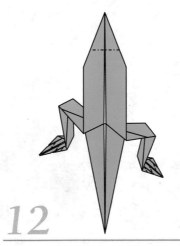

11
Make cuts (3 on each foot)
as shown.

12
Mountain fold "toes."

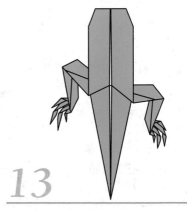

13
Completed Part 2 (rear)
of gecko.

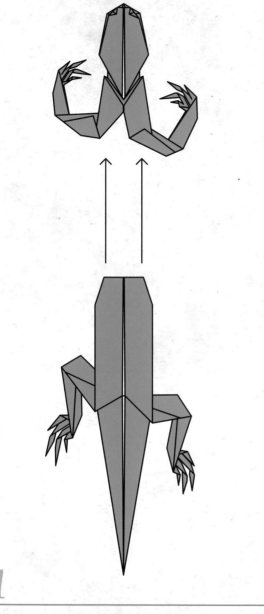

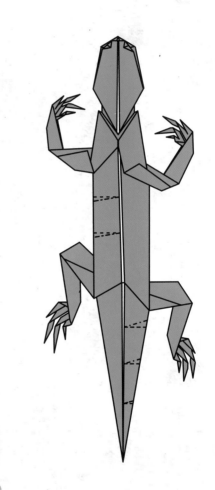

1

Join Parts 1 (front) and 2 (rear) of gecko together. Apply glue to hold.

2

Pleat fold left and right sides.

Gecko

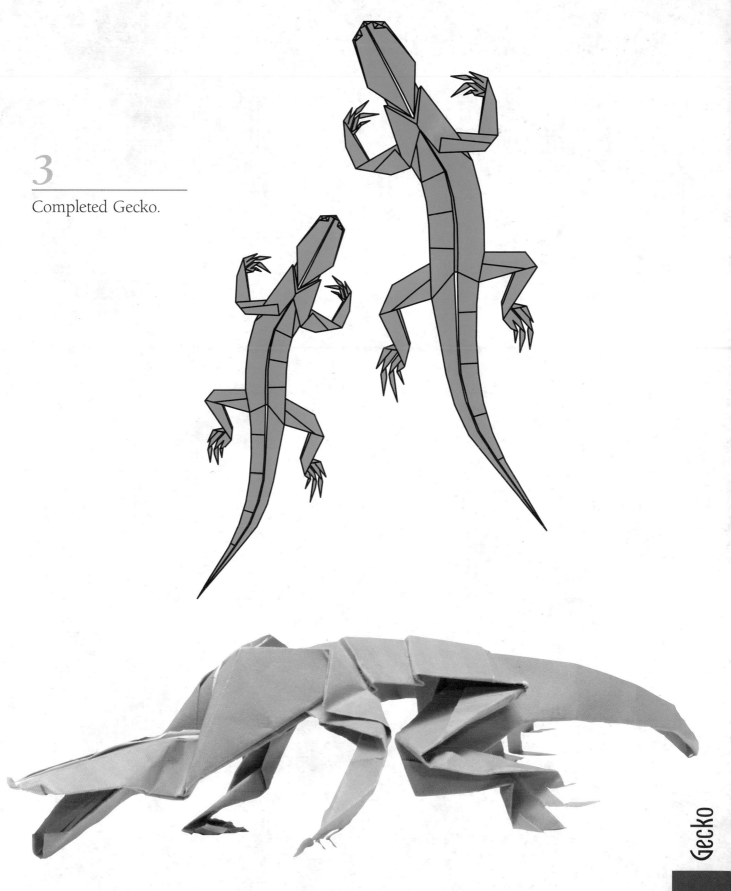

3

Completed Gecko.

Land Turtle

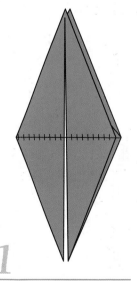

1
Start with Base Fold III. Cut as shown.

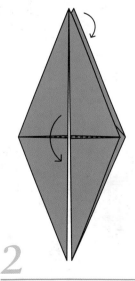

2
Valley folds both sides.

3
Inside reverse folds.

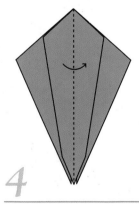

4
Valley fold.

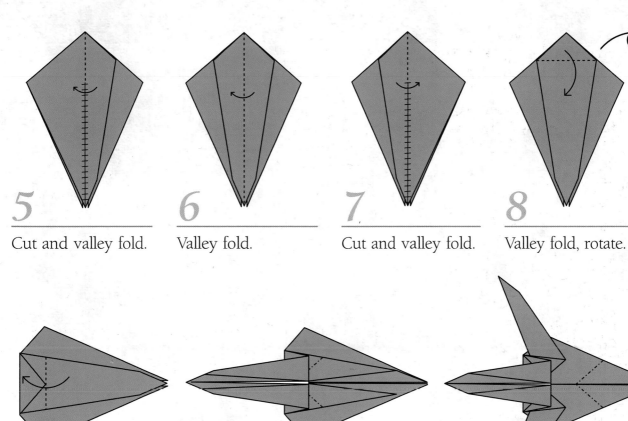

5

Cut and valley fold.

6

Valley fold.

7

Cut and valley fold.

8

Valley fold, rotate.

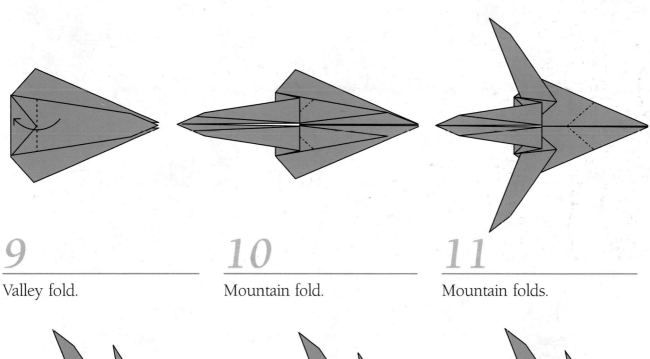

9

Valley fold.

10

Mountain fold.

11

Mountain folds.

12

Valley fold.

13

Cut and valley fold.

14

Valley fold.

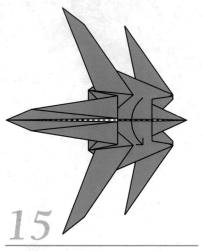

15

Valley fold in half.

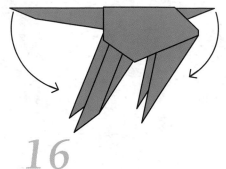

16

Pull in direction of arrow, and crimp fold into place.

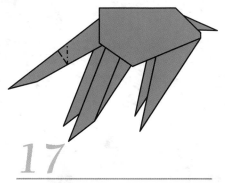

17

Pleat fold.

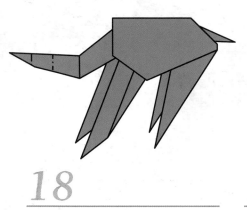

18

Pleat fold.

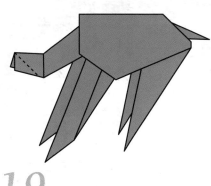

19

Valley fold both sides.

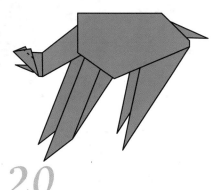

20

Valley fold both sides.

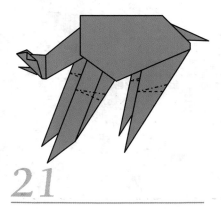

21

Pleat folds.

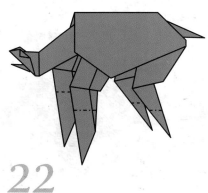

22

Inside reverse fold legs.

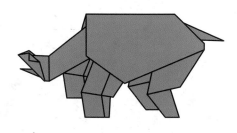

23

Push down on top and open up body.

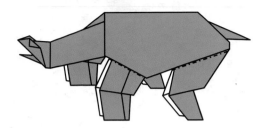

24

Mountain fold all four legs slightly inward.

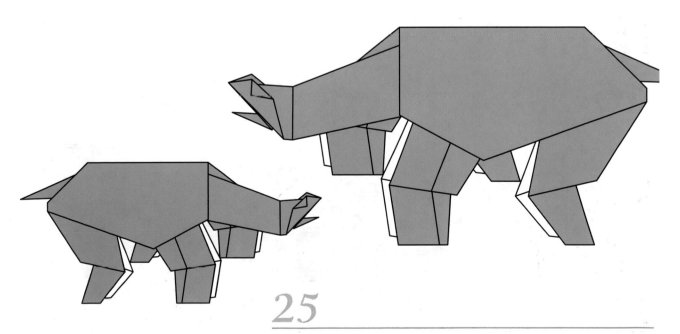

25

Completed Land Turtle.

Army Ant

Part 1

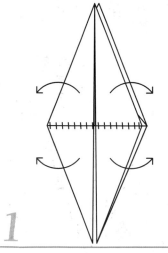

1

Start with Base Fold III.
Cuts and valley folds.

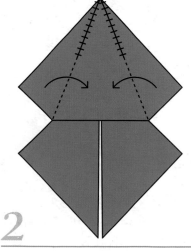

2

Cuts and valley folds.

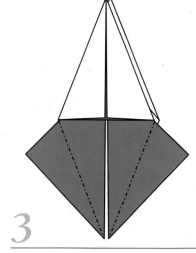

3

Mountain fold.

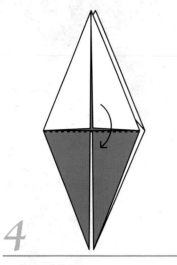

4

Valley fold.

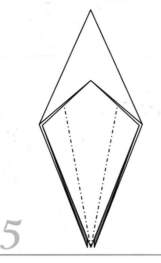

5

Inside reverse fold.

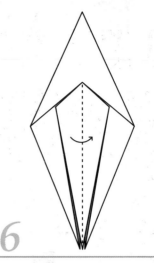

6

Valley fold.

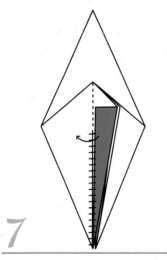

7

Cut and valley fold.

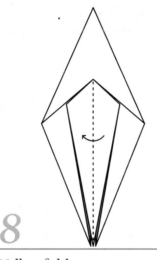

8

Valley fold.

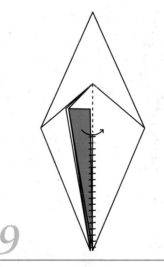

9

Cut and valley fold

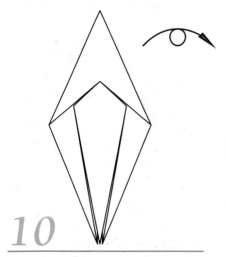

10

Turn over

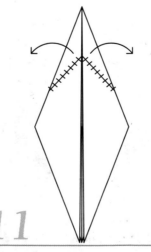

11

Cuts and valley folds.

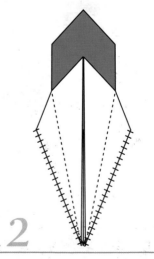

12

Repeat.

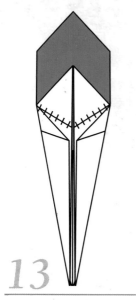

13

Cut as shown.

14

Mountain fold in half, and rotate.

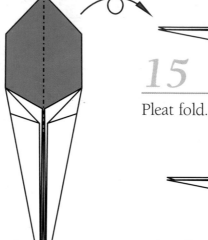

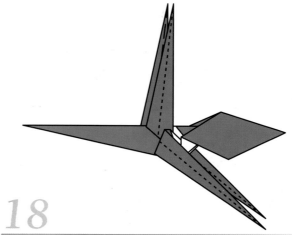

15

Pleat fold.

16

Outside reverse fold both front and back.

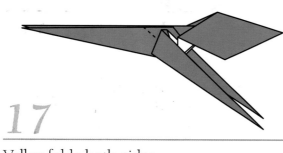

17

Valley folds both sides.

18

Valley folds both front and back.

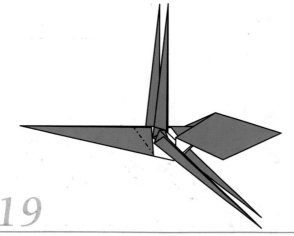

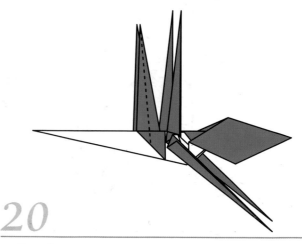

19

Inside reverse folds, front and back.

20

Valley folds both sides.

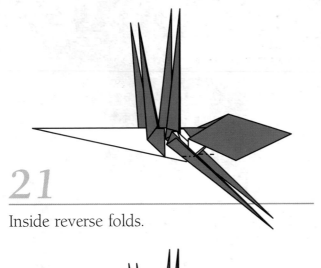

21

Inside reverse folds.

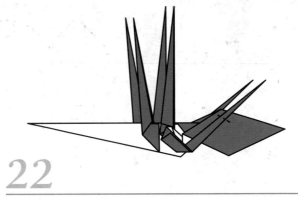

22

Inside reverse folds both sides.

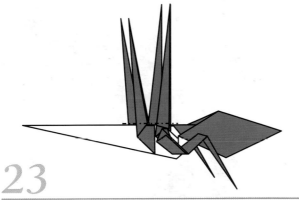

23

Repeat.

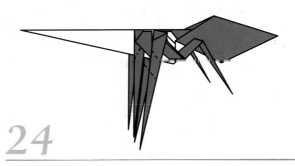

24

Pleat folds, and inside reverse both sides.

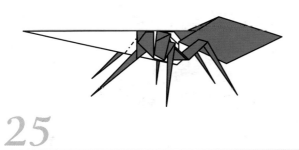

25

Inside reverse fold.

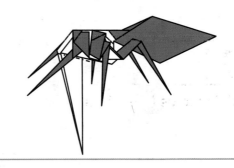

26

Inside reverse again.

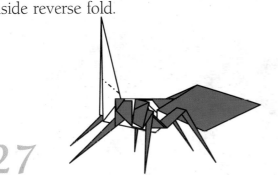

27

Inside reverse fold.

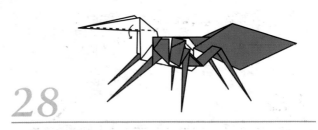

28

Valley fold both sides.

29

Cut as shown and outside reverse folds.

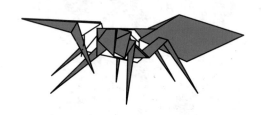

30

Mountain fold both sides.

31

Inside reverse fold both sides.

32

Valley folds.

33

Valley folds.

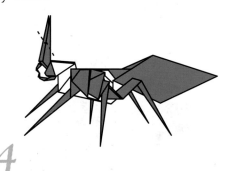

34

Valley fold both sides.

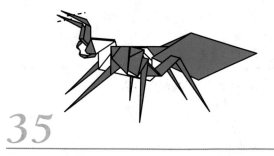

35

Mountain fold both sides.

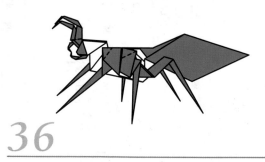

36

Valley fold both sides.

Overhead View

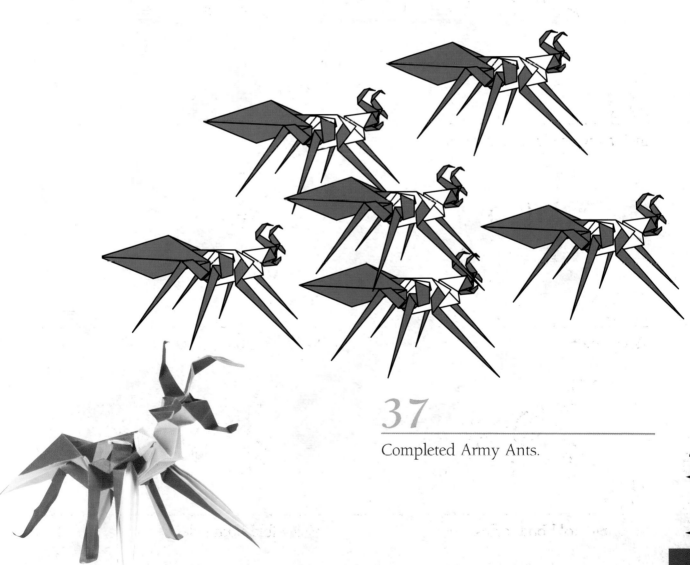

Completed Army Ants.

Komodo Dragon

Part 1

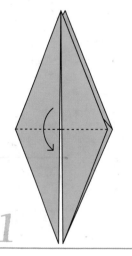

1

Start with Base Fold III, then valley fold.

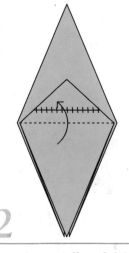

2

Cut then valley fold.

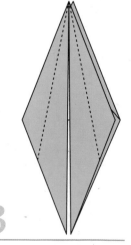

3

Valley folds.

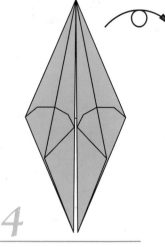

4

Turn over.

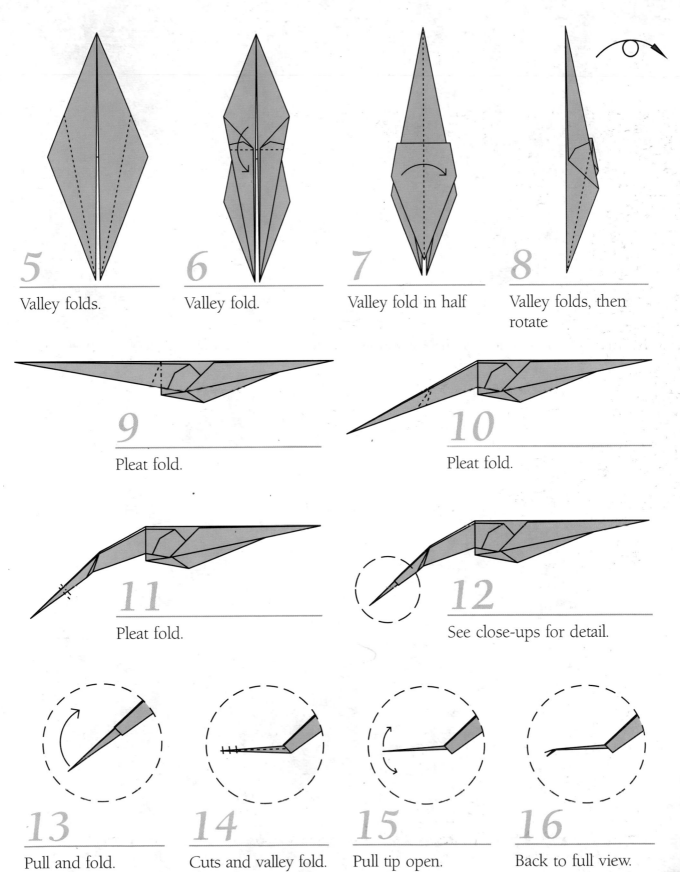

5

Valley folds.

6

Valley fold.

7

Valley fold in half

8

Valley folds, then rotate

9

Pleat fold.

10

Pleat fold.

11

Pleat fold.

12

See close-ups for detail.

13

Pull and fold.

14

Cuts and valley fold.

15

Pull tip open.

16

Back to full view.

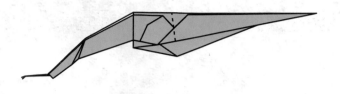

17

Valley folds both sides

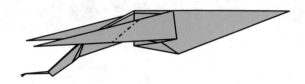

18

Inside reverse folds both sides.

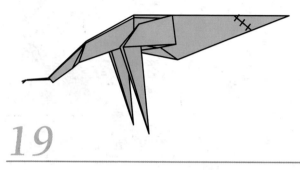

19

Cut as shown.

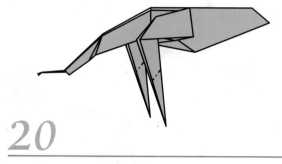

20

Inside reverse folds both sides.

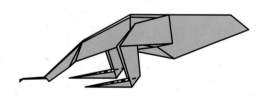

21

Mountain folds both sides.

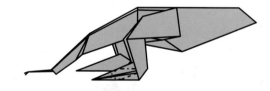

22

Squash folds both sides.

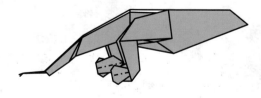

23

Mountain folds both sides.

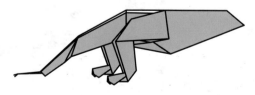

24

Complete part 1 (front) of komodo dragon.

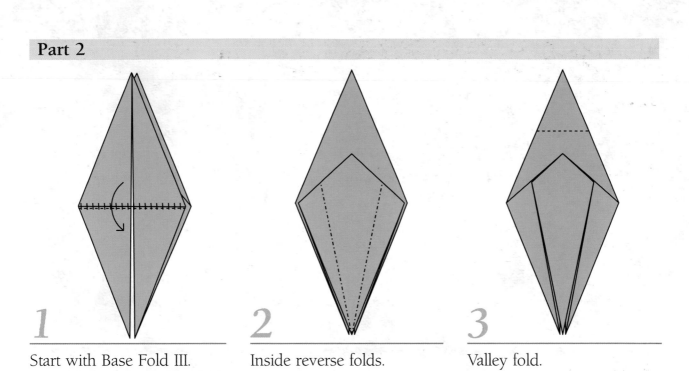

1 Start with Base Fold III.
Cuts on top layer, valley fold.

2 Inside reverse folds.

3 Valley fold.

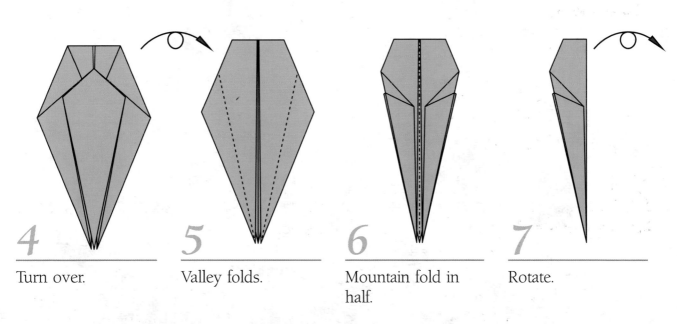

4 Turn over.

5 Valley folds.

6 Mountain fold in half.

7 Rotate.

8 Valley folds, both sides.

9 Inside reverse folds, both sides.

Komodo Dragon

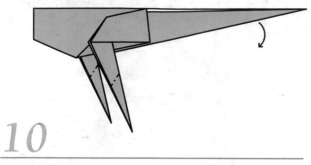

10

Inside reverse folds both sides. Pull tail into position and crimp pleat that forms inside.

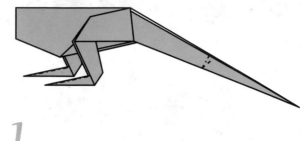

11

Mountain unfold feet; crimp tail upwards.

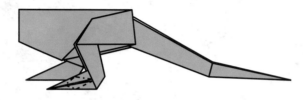

12

Squash fold both sides.

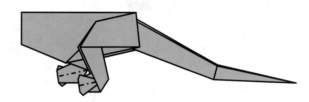

13

Mountain folds both sides.

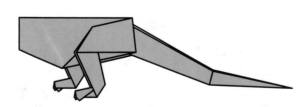

14

Complete part 2 (rear) of komodo dragon.

To Attach

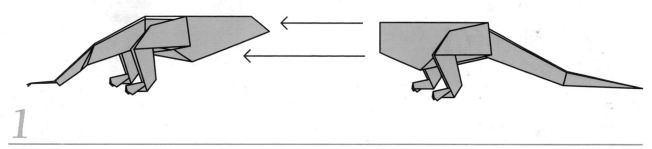

1

Join parts 1 and 2 together as shown, and apply glue to hold.

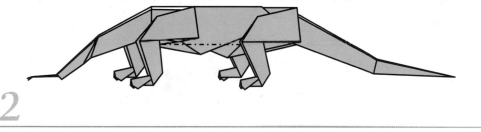

2

Mountain fold front and back.

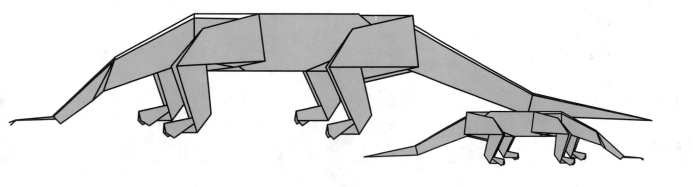

3

Completed Komodo Dragon.

Mosquito

Part 1

1

Start with Base Fold III, then valley fold both sides.

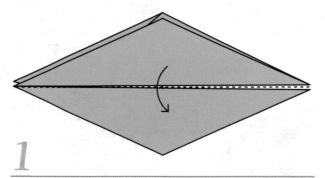

2

Cut through, then valley fold both sides.

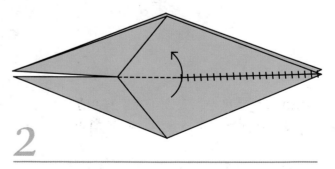

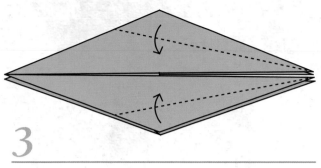

3

Valley folds to center.

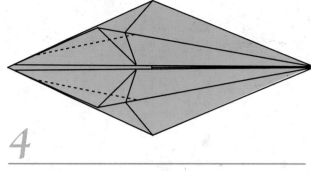

4

Valley folds.

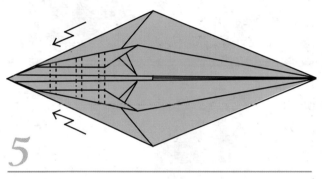

5

Pleat folds.

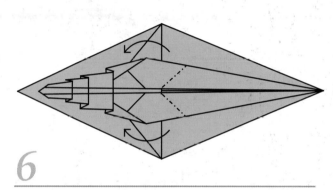

6

Mountain fold center sections out to sides.
Valley fold outside flaps to left as shown.

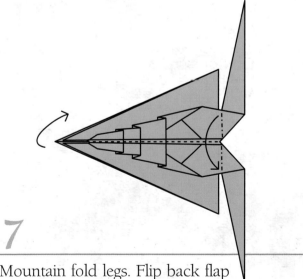

7

Mountain fold legs. Flip back flap
to right as shown. Valley fold in half.

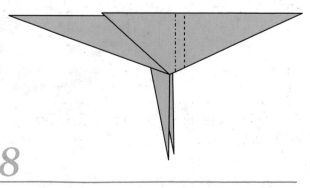

8

Pleat fold.

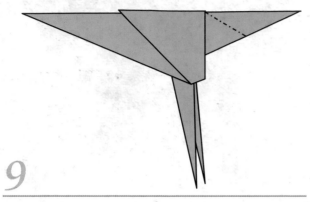

9

Inside reverse fold.

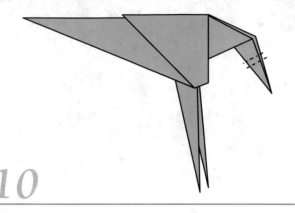

10

Pleat fold.

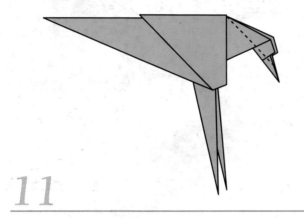

11

Valley folds both sides.

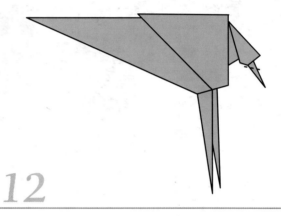

12

Outside reverse fold.

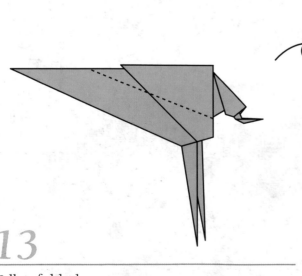

13

Valley fold, then turn over.

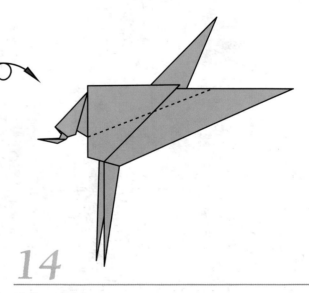

14

Valley fold.

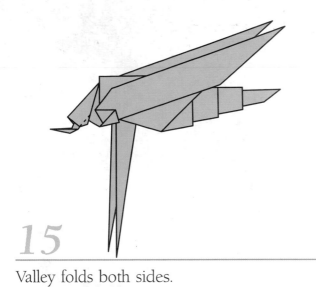

15

Valley folds both sides.

16

Complete part 1 (top) of mosquito.

Part 2

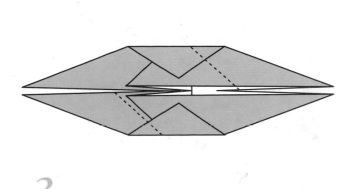

1

Start with Base Fold II, then cut as shown.

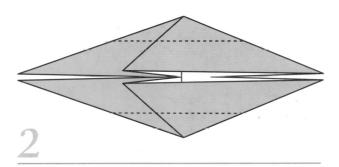

2

Valley folds.

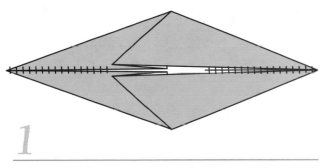

3

Valley folds.

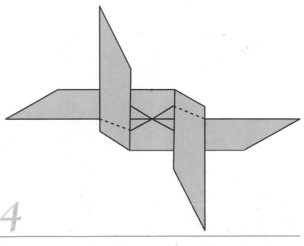

4

Repeat.

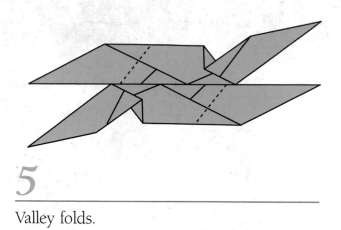

5

Valley folds.

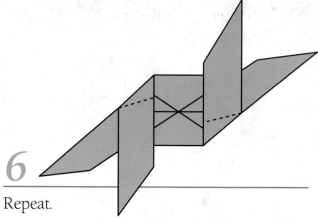

6

Repeat.

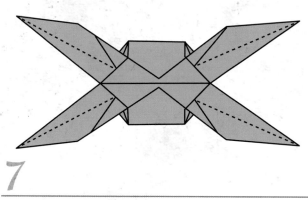

7

Squash folds.

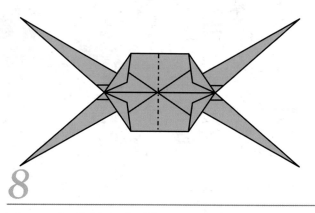

8

Mountain fold in half.

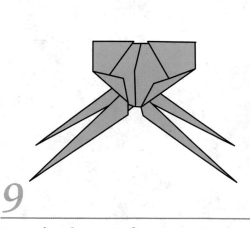

9

Completed part 2 (leg section) of mosquito.

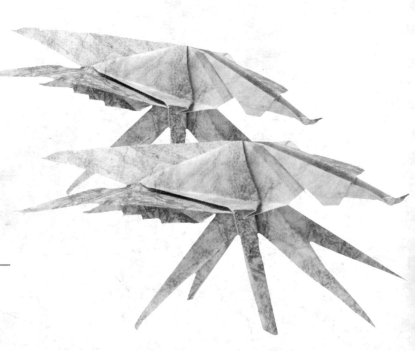

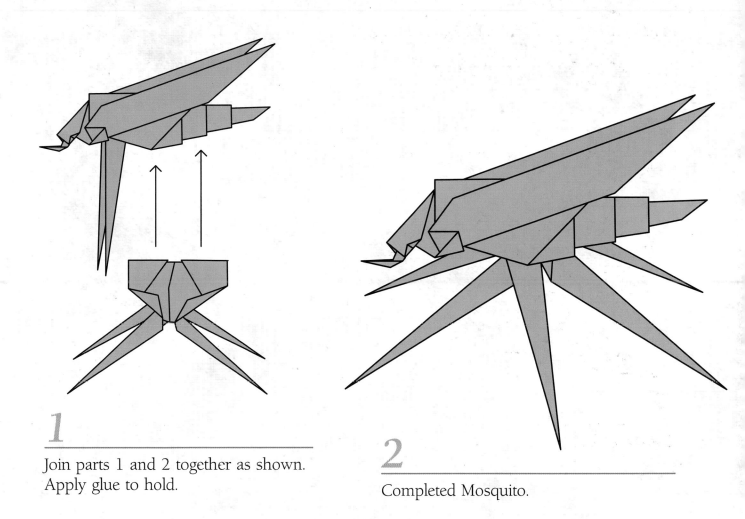

1

Join parts 1 and 2 together as shown.
Apply glue to hold.

2

Completed Mosquito.

Mosquito

Praying Mantis

Part 1

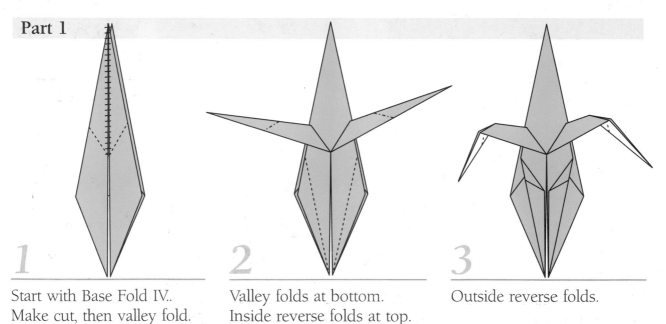

1
Start with Base Fold IV..
Make cut, then valley fold.

2
Valley folds at bottom.
Inside reverse folds at top.

3
Outside reverse folds.

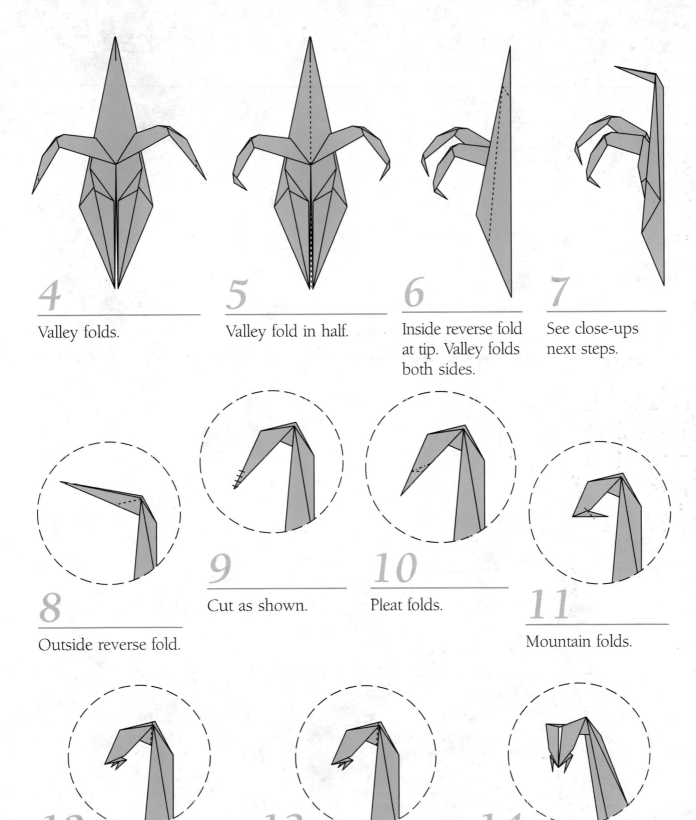

4
Valley folds.

5
Valley fold in half.

6
Inside reverse fold
at tip. Valley folds
both sides.

7
See close-ups
next steps.

8
Outside reverse fold.

9
Cut as shown.

10
Pleat folds.

11
Mountain folds.

12
Fold then unfold.

13
Squash fold.

14
Back to full view.

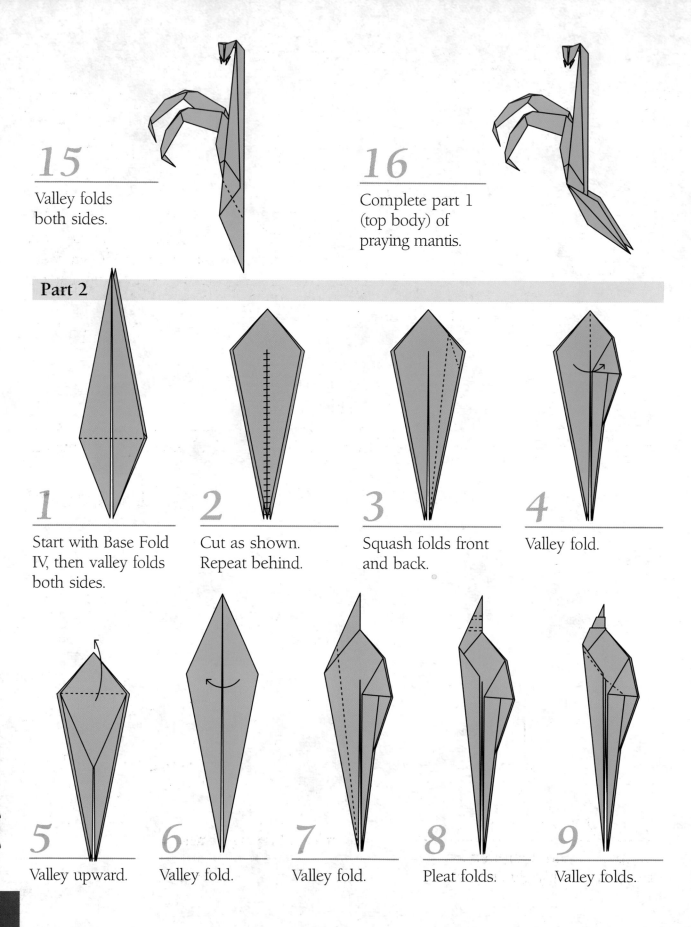

15

Valley folds both sides.

16

Complete part 1 (top body) of praying mantis.

Part 2

1

Start with Base Fold IV, then valley folds both sides.

2

Cut as shown. Repeat behind.

3

Squash folds front and back.

4

Valley fold.

5

Valley upward.

6

Valley fold.

7

Valley fold.

8

Pleat folds.

9

Valley folds.

Praying Mantis

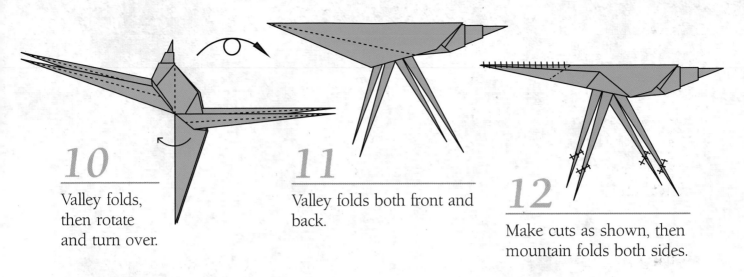

10
Valley folds, then rotate and turn over.

11
Valley folds both front and back.

12
Make cuts as shown, then mountain folds both sides.

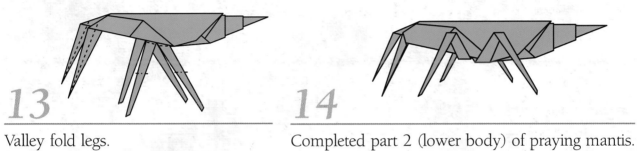

13
Valley fold legs.

14
Completed part 2 (lower body) of praying mantis.

To Attach

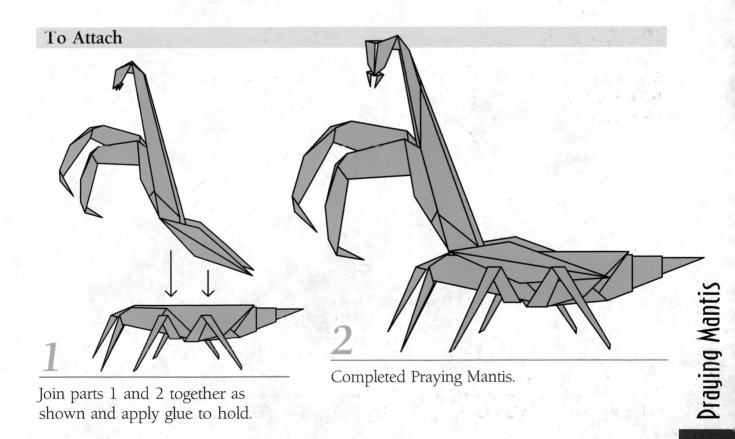

1
Join parts 1 and 2 together as shown and apply glue to hold.

2
Completed Praying Mantis.

Wasp

Part 1

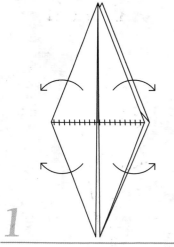

1

Start with Base fold III. Cut front layer, then valley fold.

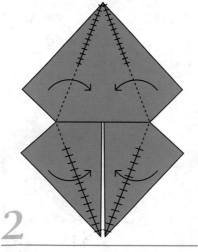

2

Cuts and valley folds.

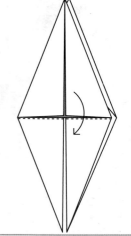

3

Valley fold.

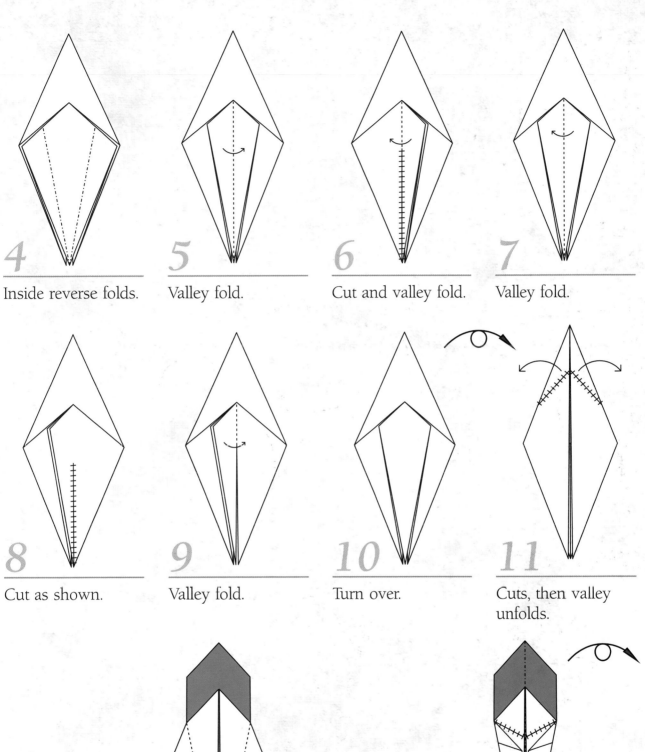

4

Inside reverse folds.

5

Valley fold.

6

Cut and valley fold.

7

Valley fold.

8

Cut as shown.

9

Valley fold.

10

Turn over.

11

Cuts, then valley unfolds.

12

Cuts and valley folds.

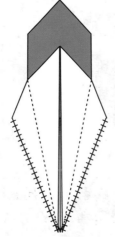

13

Cuts as shown, then mountain fold in half. Rotate.

14

Outside reverse fold.

15

Outside reverse fold.

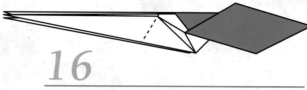

16

Outside reverse folds front and back.

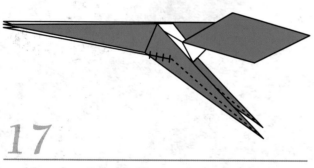

17

Cuts and valley folds front and back.

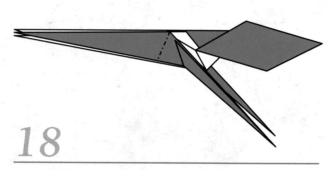

18

Mountain folds both sides.

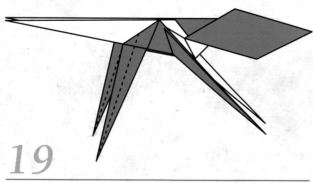

19

Valley folds both sides.

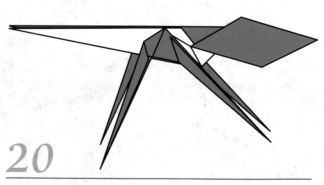

20

Valley fold both inner layers (hidden) of sections at left (see next step).

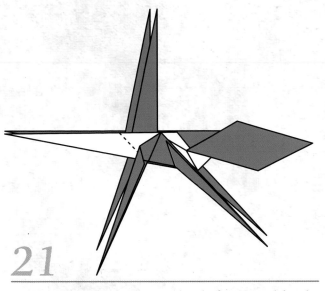

21

Now valley outer layers both front and back.

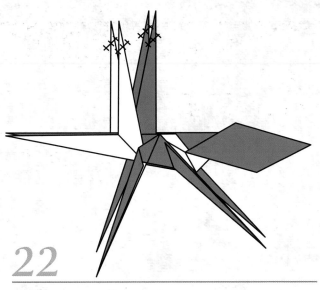

22

Make cuts as shown.

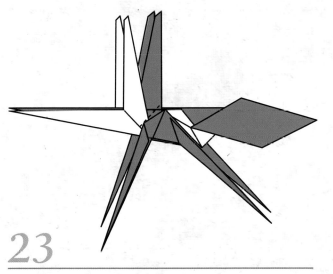

23

Valley fold wing sections front and back.

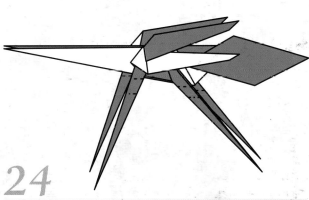

24

Pleat fold all legs.

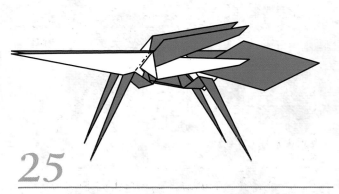

25

Inside reverse fold.

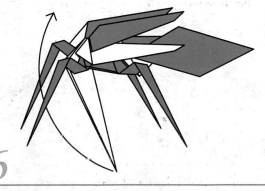

26

Inside reverse fold as shown by arrow.

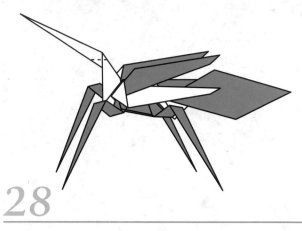

27

Inside reverse fold.

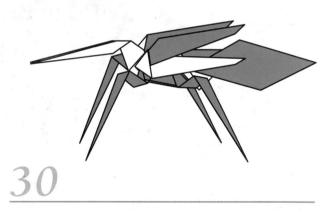

28

Outside reverse fold.

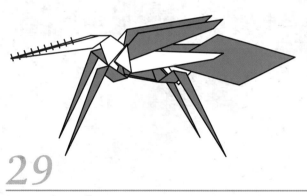

29

Make cut as shown.

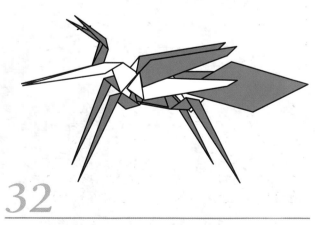

30

Valley fold both inner layers (hidden) of section at left (see next step).

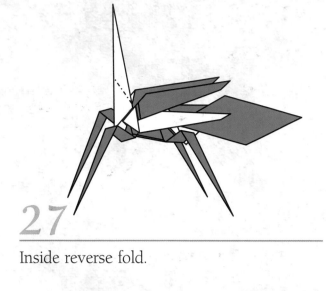

31

Valley fold both front and back.

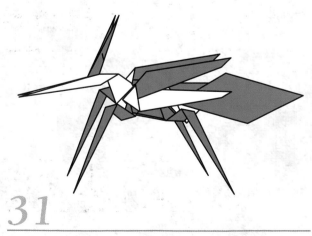

32

Mountain fold both front and back.

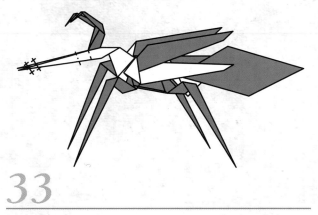

33

Make cuts as shown, then mirror pleat fold both sides

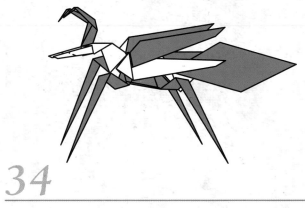

34

Mountain folds both sides

35

Complete part 1 (body) of wasp.

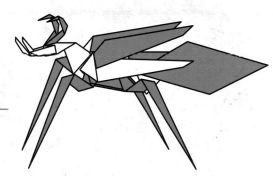

Part 2

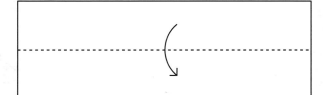

1

As with the Dragonfly, for the legs start with an 8.5" by 2.5" strip of paper—the amount left from a letter-size sheet once an 8.5" square is removed. Valley fold.

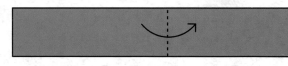

2

Valley fold.

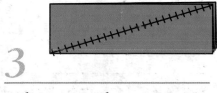

3

Make cuts as shown.

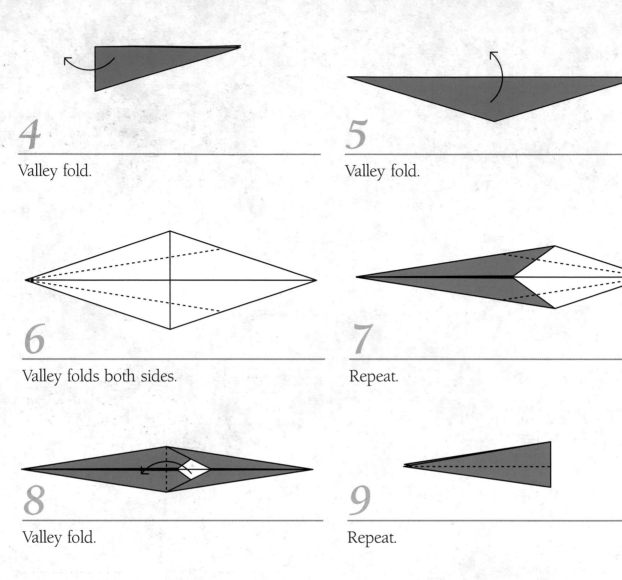

4

Valley fold.

5

Valley fold.

6

Valley folds both sides.

7

Repeat.

8

Valley fold.

9

Repeat.

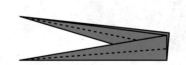

10

Pull and fold.

11

Valley folds.

12

Completed part 2 (central legs) of wasp.

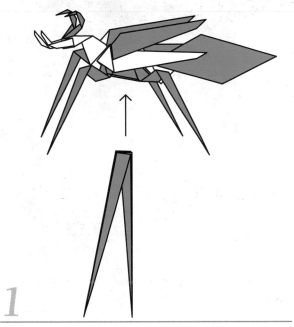

1

Join part 2 (legs) to part 1 (body), and apply glue to hold.

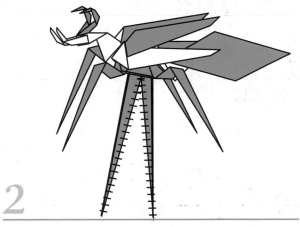

2

Make cuts as shown.

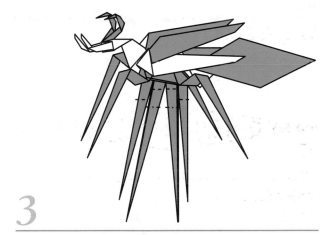

3

Pleat fold center leg sets both sides.

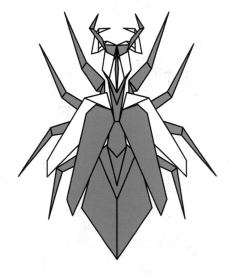

Overhead View

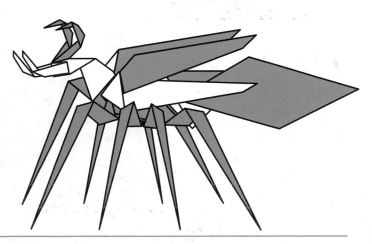

4

Completed Wasp.

Sea Turtle

1

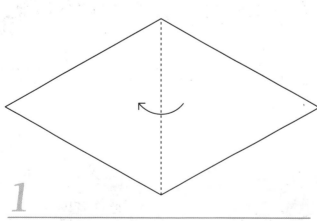

Use rectangular sheet of paper approximately 8" by 11" size (29.5 by 28 cm), do Base Fold IV up to step 6.

2

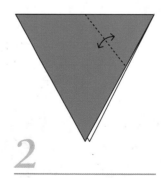

Fold then unfold.

3

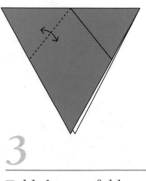

Fold then unfold.

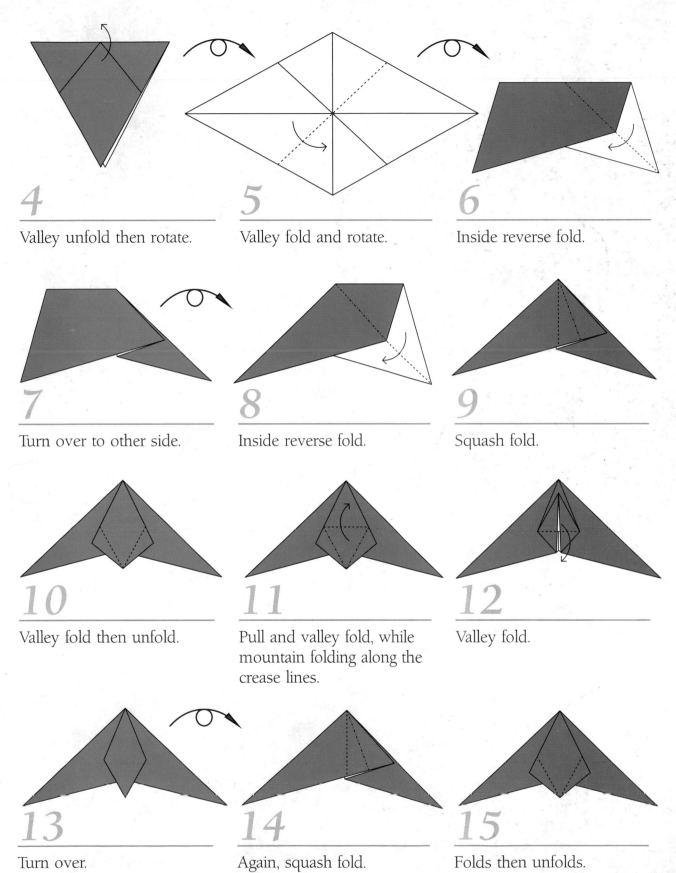

4

Valley unfold then rotate.

5

Valley fold and rotate.

6

Inside reverse fold.

7

Turn over to other side.

8

Inside reverse fold.

9

Squash fold.

10

Valley fold then unfold.

11

Pull and valley fold, while mountain folding along the crease lines.

12

Valley fold.

13

Turn over.

14

Again, squash fold.

15

Folds then unfolds.

Sea Turtle

16
Pull and valley fold.

17
Valley fold.

18
Valley fold.

19
Squash fold.

20
Folds then unfolds.

21
Pull and valley fold.

22
Valley fold.

23
Turn over to other side.

24
Valley fold.

25
Squash fold.

26
Repeat steps 20 to 22.

27
Valley fold.

28
Valley fold and unfold.

29
Unfold completely.

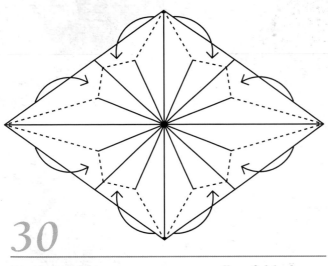

30

Pinch together at corners to valley fold along dashed lines.

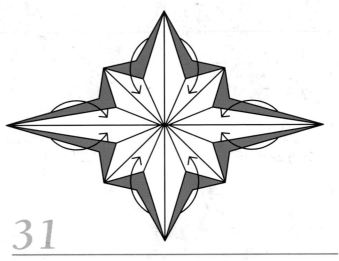

31

Appearance just before completion.

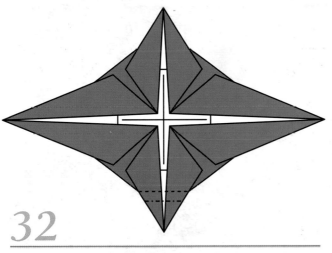

32

Pleat fold.

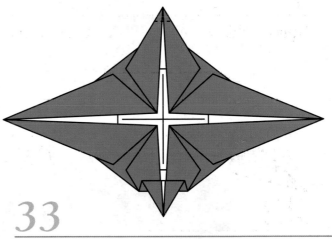

33

Valley fold.

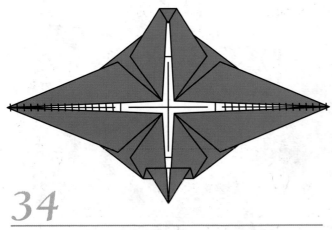

34

Make cuts as shown.

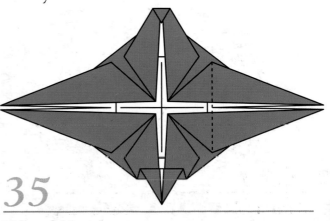

35

Valley folds.

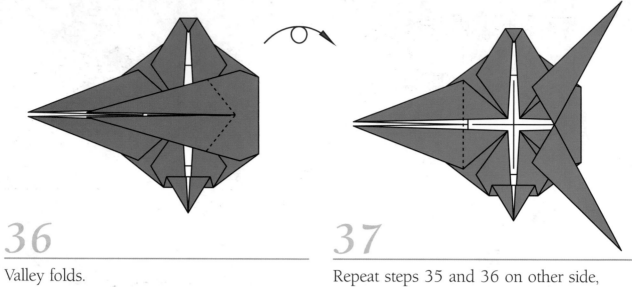

36

Valley folds.

37

Repeat steps 35 and 36 on other side, then rotate.

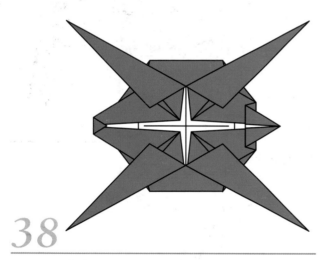

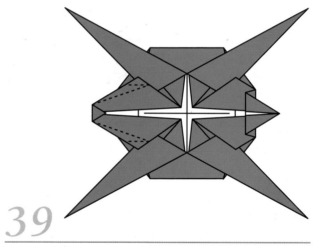

38

Secure all four legs under head and tail.

39

Valley folds and squash folds both sides.

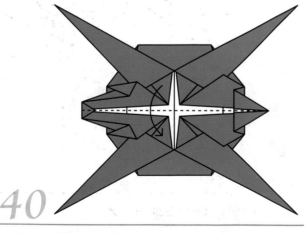

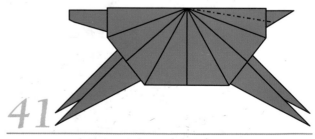

40

Valley fold in half.

41

Inside reverse fold (glue to hold).

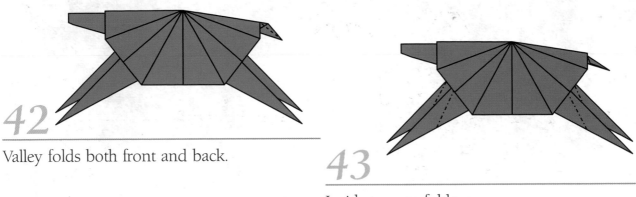

42

Valley folds both front and back.

43

Inside reverse folds.

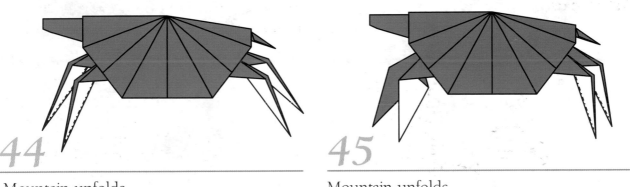

44

Mountain unfolds.

45

Mountain unfolds.

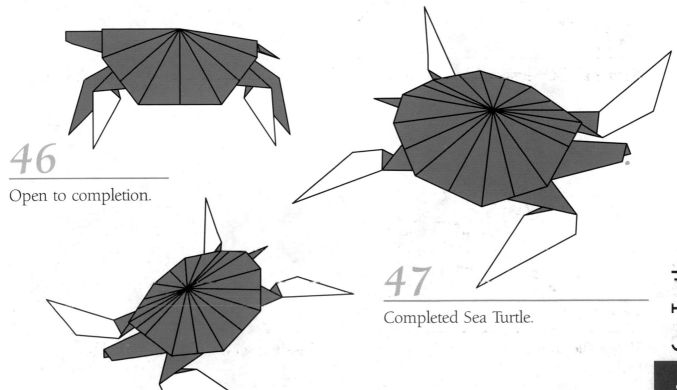

46

Open to completion.

47

Completed Sea Turtle.

Tarantula

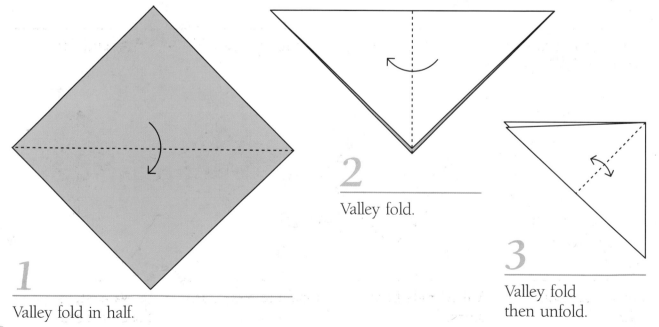

1

Valley fold in half.

2

Valley fold.

3

Valley fold
then unfold.

4

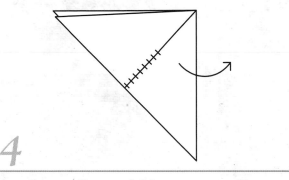

Cut then valley unfold.

5

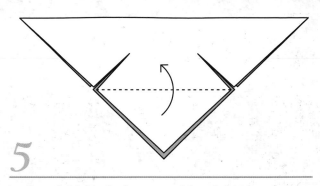

Valley fold both front and back.

6

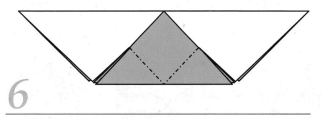

Inside reverse folds.

7

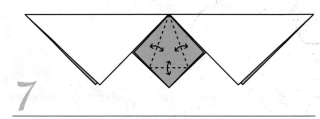

Valley folds and unfolds.

8

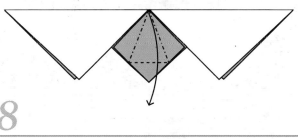

Pull tip in direction of arrow and valley fold, mountain folding on creases. Repeat behind.

9

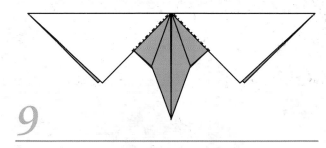

Inside reverse folds both right and left.

10

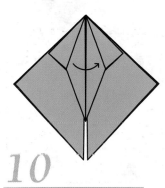

Valley folds both sides.

11

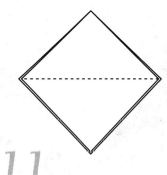

Valley folds both sides.

12

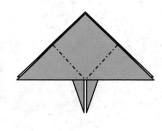

Inside reverse folds.

13

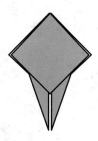

See next steps for close-up detail.

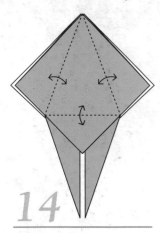

14

Valley fold then unfold both front and back.

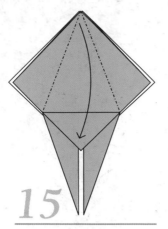

15

Pull tip and fold on crease lines front and back.

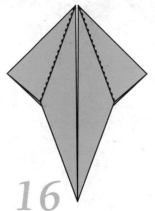

16

Valley folds and unfolds.

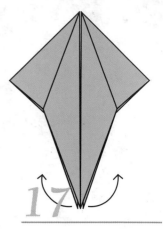

17

Pull open to flatten (see step 19).

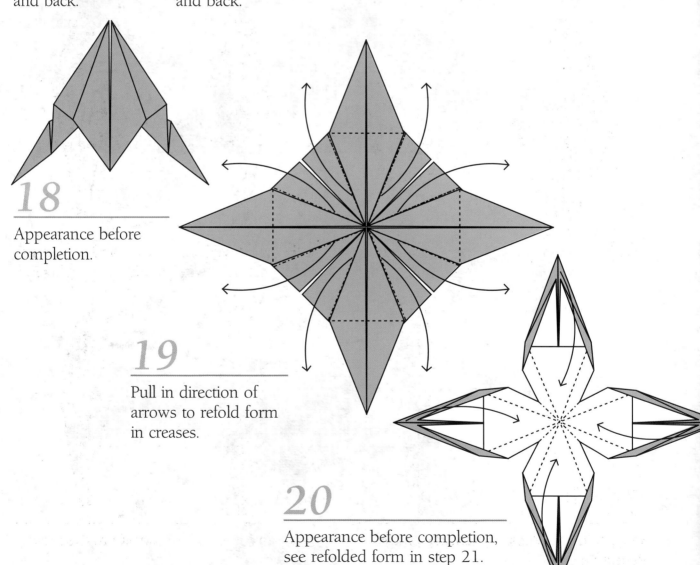

18

Appearance before completion.

19

Pull in direction of arrows to refold form in creases.

20

Appearance before completion, see refolded form in step 21.

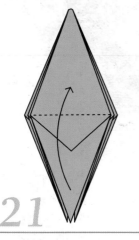

21

Refolded form, now valley folds.

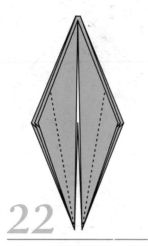

22

Valley folds.

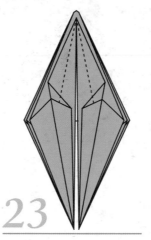

23

Valley folds.

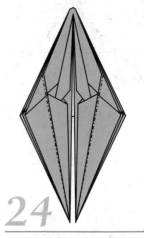

24

Mountain folds.

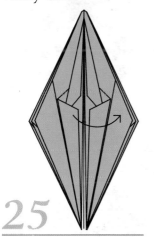

25

Valley fold twice.

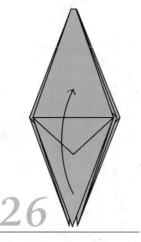

26

Repeat steps 21 to 24 on other sides.

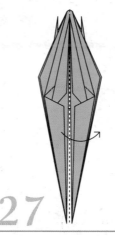

27

Valley fold twice.

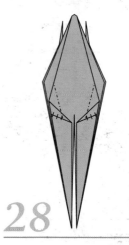

28

Cuts and mountain folds. Repeat behind.

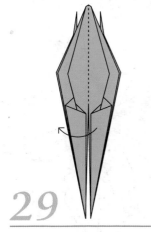

29

Valley fold four flaps. Repeat behind.

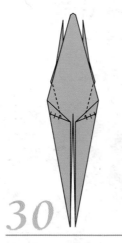

30

Repeat step 28.

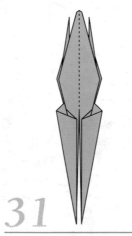

31

Valley fold.

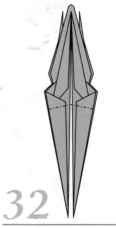

32

Inside reverse folds.

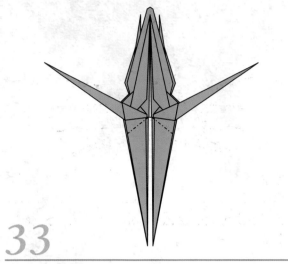

33

Inside reverse folds.

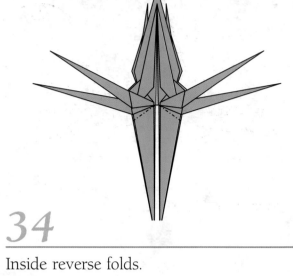

34

Inside reverse folds.

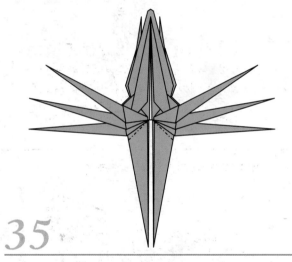

35

Inside reverse folds.

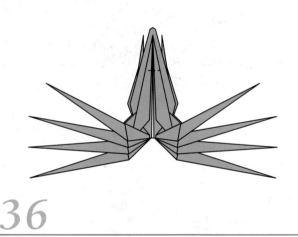

36

Valley fold tip.

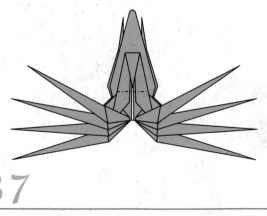

37

Mountain fold.

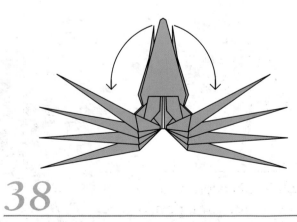

38

Inside reverse folds in direction of arrows.

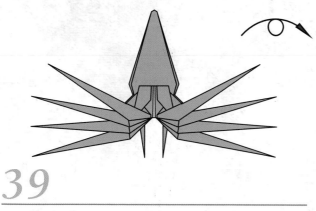

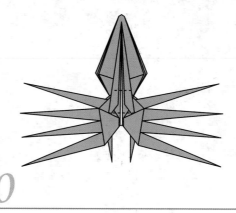

39

Turn over to other side.

40

Valley fold twice, and apply glue to tip for holding.

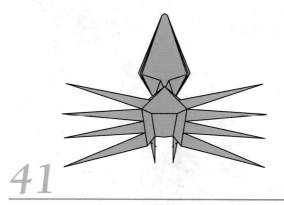

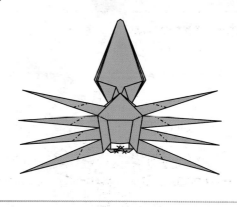

41

Outside reverse folds.

42

Cuts, then mountain fold all legs.

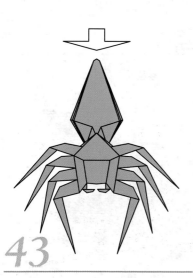

43

Push in direction of arrow to open out form, position legs naturally.

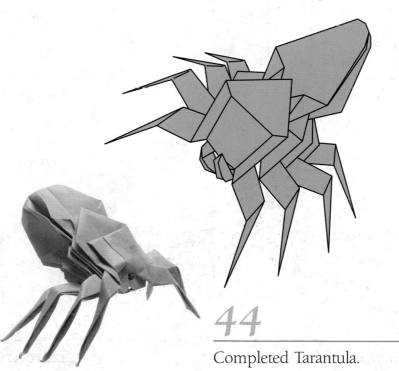

44

Completed Tarantula.

Komodo dragon

Dragonfly

Gallery of Creepy Crawlies

Gecko

Tarantula

Sea turtle

Lobster

Army ants

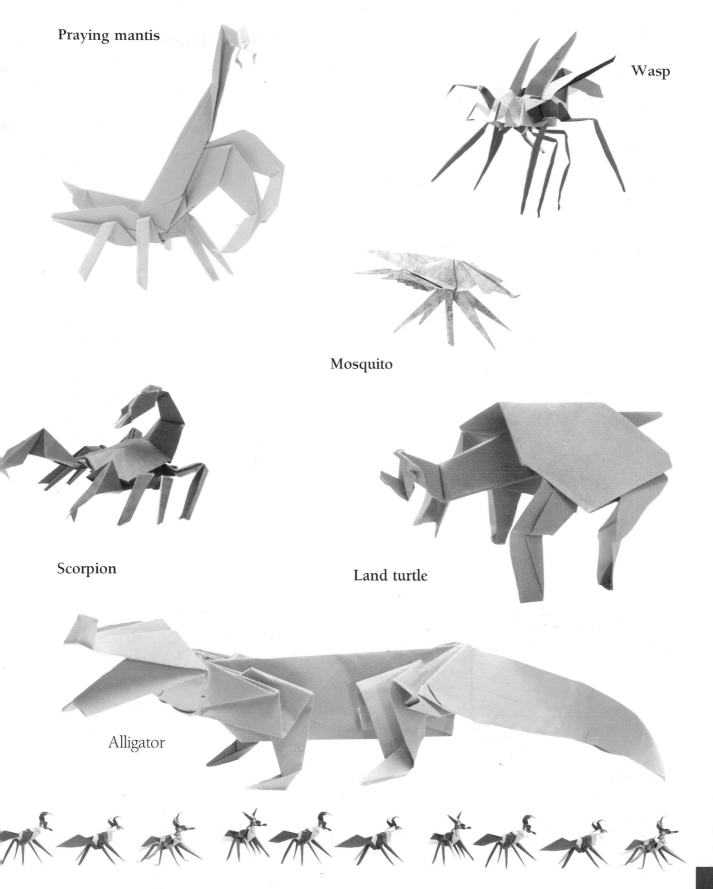

Praying mantis

Wasp

Mosquito

Scorpion

Land turtle

Alligator

Index